W9-AAI-133

THE UNHOLY TRINITY

THE
UNHOLY
TRINITY

**BLOCKING THE LEFT'S
ASSAULT ON LIFE, MARRIAGE,
AND GENDER**

Matt Walsh

IMAGE

NEW YORK

Copyright © 2017 by Matt Walsh

All rights reserved.
Published in the United States by Image, an imprint of the
Crown Publishing Group, a division of Penguin Random House
LLC, New York.
crownpublishing.com

Image is a registered trademark and the "I" colophon is a trademark
of Penguin Random House LLC.

Library of Congress Cataloging-in-Publication Data is available
upon request.

ISBN 978-0-451-49505-1
Ebook ISBN 978-0-451-49506-8

Printed in the United States of America

10 9 8 7 6 5 4 3 2 1

First Edition

CONTENTS

1. Born in Hell 1

2. The High Sacrament 13

3. The Autonomy Myth 44

4. The Death Cult 67

5. The Abandonment of Marriage 85

6. The Impossibility of Same-Sex
   Marriage 101

7. Acceptance Is Mandatory 131

8. The Insanity of Transgenderism 150

9. The Scourge of Feminism 176

10. The Inequality of the Sexes 199

11. The Darkest Night 217

   Acknowledgments 231

Born in Hell

LIBERALISM AS SELF-WORSHIP, AND
HOW IT'S REDEFINING REALITY
FOR EVERYONE

The first liberal was named Lucifer. He was an angel. He lived in Heaven millennia ago, before modern times, before ancient times, before time itself. He could still be there today if that's what he'd chosen, but in his absurd and insatiable pride he would not bend his knee to the supreme will of God.

Non serviam. "I will not serve," he said, wanting to love only himself.

Just like that, he and those who followed him were cast out of Paradise, down into the hideous depths of Hell, where he could reign over his pitiful kingdom of darkness. It was there, in the fires of damnation, that the philosophy of liberalism was born, although it wouldn't be known by that name for many years. I'm telling a somewhat abbreviated version of the story, I realize.

It was this philosophy that led to the Fall of Man, when Adam and Eve succumbed to the temptations of the serpent and attempted to make themselves equal to God.

It was the philosophy behind every act of human evil throughout history, at the bottom of every atrocity. It's the philosophy you would have found incubating in Sodom and Gomorrah amid the orgy of heathens, or in the Temple of Baal, where the pagans made human sacrifices as part of their barbaric fertility rituals, and to ensure for themselves wealth and prosperity.

This philosophy has propelled all the great villains throughout history. It is the philosophy of Judas, of Nero, of Genghis Khan, of Adolf Hitler, of Hillary Clinton. The specifics of what these people all believed, and how they framed it around the political circumstances of the day, isn't terribly relevant, for they desired the same thing and worshipped the same god: the self.

What we call "liberalism" in public discourse today is really just the worship of self. It is the categorical belief in the supremacy of the individual. The particulars of modern American liberalism, or progressivism if you like, were certainly informed by the social, political, religious, and sexual philosophies of Machiavelli, Kant, Nietzsche, Freud, Marx, and Sartre—the "pillars of unbelief," as Peter Kreeft calls them—as well as guys like Kinsey and Singer, but underpinning everything is a studied and intentional selfishness.

Of course, we all lapse into selfishness at times—I often provide proof of that—but those who affirm the ultimate primacy of the self all share the same ideology. Their worship might manifest itself in different ways, but they're all cut from the same cloth woven by the Devil himself eons ago.

You can find this philosophy anywhere, and not just coming out of the mouths of people who identify as "liberals." You can find it in our churches, in our schools, in our homes, on TV. You can find it tucked away under slogans—tolerance, acceptance, etc.—that sound quite noble at first blush.

FAUX VIRTUES

In classical times, the Greeks ordered their ethical universe around four cardinal virtues: prudence, justice, temperance, and courage. The Church later added three more that Paul had highlighted in his first letter to the Corinthians: faith, hope, and love. It wasn't until the late twentieth century that noted modern philosophers like

Lady Gaga and Barney the Dinosaur promoted tolerance and acceptance as not just cardinal virtues but the only virtues.

It seems that nobody really talks about courage, or justice, or faith anymore. There is, apparently, no need to act bravely or seek justice so long as we are tolerant and accepting. And I can't help but notice that the people who prattle on the loudest about those two faux virtues almost always do so self-servingly. They aren't asking that we tolerate and accept *everything*—even they believe some things are still intolerable and unacceptable, such as Nazism and Orthodox Christianity—just that we tolerate and accept whatever it is that they themselves are doing at the time.

Of course, even when tolerance and acceptance are promoted and celebrated more broadly and nonspecifically, it is still, in the end, selfish. The seven virtues advanced by the ancient Greeks and the early Church fathers require action and self-denial. For example, if I insist that people behave temperately, I have just burdened myself with the same expectation. I could shout for temperance in between monster bong hits and Cheetos binges, but then I would make myself a hypocrite. Better to explicitly dismiss temperance and any other difficult, sacrificial virtue, and instead advance virtues that I can live out and demonstrate without changing my lifestyle at all. Thus I turn to tolerance and acceptance.

It takes nothing to tolerate and accept. I can incorporate tolerance and acceptance into my bong hits and Cheetos routine. I can incorporate it into anything. Indeed, the more indulgent and lazy I become, the more apt I am to tolerate and accept. It takes effort and work to not tolerate something. Tolerance, on the other hand, just requires me to sit back and mind my own business. It becomes, then, a win-win for liberals. They can live however they want, do whatever they want, be as selfish as they want, and far from experiencing any sort of guilt or remorse, they can actually feel quite proud of themselves.

BECAUSE I'M ME

Self-worship has become the predominant religion in our culture. It is why we, as a society, have caved in on ourselves, like dying stars, and are now sucking each other into the black hole of our megalomania. We can't see the world outside the window, because we're too busy whispering sweet nothings to our reflections in the glass.

There is a hierarchy of beings in the universe, with God sitting all the way at the unattainable apex of it. But when God is dethroned and the existence of all heavenly and spiritual entities denied, man is left suddenly at the peak of the pyramid. Now we are the pinnacle. Or, at the very least, the pinnacle is in reach, and our goal is now to claim it. To become the Übermensch as Nietzsche described, before he was admitted to a mental hospital and later died diseased and insane.

If we are, or can become, the apogee of all reality, then we are the only ones deserving of our worship. We should adore and praise ourselves simply because we are ourselves. This is the message embedded into most of what we ingest in music, films, and television, and it is the message explicitly taught to us from a young age.

I can still recall the insufferable "self-esteem" seminars we were subjected to in grade school. I remember my teacher telling us that we all ought to hold ourselves in enormously high esteem, because we're great and special and there is nobody in the world more spectacular than us. I found this a peculiar statement at the time, particularly coming from the woman who'd just given me a D on my last math quiz. I asked *why* I should so venerate myself.

"Because you're special!"

"But what's special about me?"

"You're you!"

The correct answer is that I'm special because I am a child of God. But our culture has ruled God out, leaving us with the only alternative explanation: I'm special because, for all intents and purposes, I am god.

THE MIGHTY ME

The proponents of this philosophy, those we call "liberal," believe that the individual is supreme. There is no power or authority above the Mighty Me; therefore, nothing has the right to impose itself on Me, and nothing—not my child, not my biology, not the law, not institutions, not even reality—can hold any claim over me. Nothing has or can exercise a right to *my* life or *my* body or *my* love or *my* time. My, Me, I. I am the sole point and purpose of the universe, and the highest thing I can hope to attain is my own enjoyment, convenience, and pleasure. There is no truth outside of that. There is no God beyond myself.

According to the liberal—the secular Satanist, you might call him—each person is a Me, a Mighty Me, and all values and morals are hollowed out and reduced to serve Me. I am entirely autonomous and sovereign, and everything is relative to Me. I make my own truth, my own science, my own universe. This is what Satan set out to do, and the universe he created was the nothingness of Hell, a Hell that the modern liberal wants desperately to join.

This is why, as you'll see in this book, liberalism is utterly preoccupied with sex. Sex is, quite simply, the most powerful force in our nature. It is a spring of great beauty and wonder. But it is also the most potent danger—the source, throughout human history and mythology, of humanity's sin and downfall.

The modern heresies of relativism, feminism, and materialism trade—and prosper—on this paradox, as their author, Satan, well comprehends.

He has used it since the dawn of time to entice humans away from God. And arguably, Satan has never enjoyed a more productive period than our own in which to try and "win" his argument against God. Sex, turned upside down and shaken until it is empty of all morality, quickly becomes an obsession, and to appease the obsession the sex becomes more radical and perverse.

When a person worships the self and lives in a culture like ours, where the self reigns above all, all that's really left to do and think about is sex. And, as we'll see, death. Sex and death. When you are not pursuing a virtuous life or seeking spiritual fulfillment of any kind, all the Mighty Me can do is please itself—and die.

Of course, living in a society where everyone is a god can get tricky. It should be noted here that, according to the dictates of our culture, every other Mighty Me can live in his or her own bubble of self-gratification and self-worship, and if two Mes happen to bump into one another, it's best if they're polite in order to avoid a battle of egos. This is why, the liberal would say, the Bible tells us to "love your neighbor as yourself."

They take this verse to mean that self-love is the

highest love, and that we ought to usually treat others fairly as a matter of pragmatism, because it makes us feel good to be treated fairly too. They miss the whole rest of Scripture, including the line just before that, which says rather definitively, "Love the Lord your God with all your heart and with all your soul and with all your mind and with all your strength." The *second* most important commandment, as Jesus outlines in the Gospel of Mark, is "Love your neighbor as yourself."

Liberalism/Satanism removes God from that equation, striking the first commandment entirely and destroying the context for the second, leaving only the self, which cuts off the source and purpose of the love, turning it against itself.

That's why the other Mes don't always have to be afforded respect or even basic human dignity. The moment one of them becomes a burden—the moment they ask us to change or give or serve or love in any sort of active way—is when they transform into a parasite to be extracted and discarded. The ultimate example of this is abortion. We, the Mighty Mes, think nothing of attempting to extend our lives by cannibalizing our own children. After all, I am Me, the one true God, and what greater cause could there be than prolonging my own existence?

A THREE-PRONGED ATTACK

I'm not trying to simply fling insults at liberals by accusing them of being Satanists in league with the Devil (but I guess I'm not complimenting them, either). The Satanism of the modern liberal is almost always latent and secular, not theological. What I'm trying to establish is that the prevailing philosophy of our culture is rooted in an evil that can be traced back to the beginning of everything. This is not new, we should realize.

I use the terms *liberal* and *progressive* and *liberalism* and *progressivism* simply because these are the names and labels we place on the contemporary manifestation of this ancient evil. But it doesn't actually matter what name you use. You could call a liberal a "progressive," a "banana," or an "oogliebooglie"—it's the belief system, not the labels, we'll be dealing with in this book.

The wicked brilliance of modern liberalism is that it knows everyone must live in a relativistic society in order for the individual to truly be deified, and in a relativistic society, *everything* must be relative. And so their three-pronged attack on life, marriage, and gender began. The liberalism of today can be defined by its single-minded insistence on defining and redefining everything. To let something maintain its own definition, to accept something for what it is, would be to surrender our autonomy. Therefore, the liberal can let nothing be what it is. Least of all life, marriage, and gender.

The liberal assault on these three fronts—the titular Unholy Trinity—serves as the foundation for everything else in their agenda. Whatever political or social issues people debate on Twitter and Facebook these days, all of them begin here. If our culture can successfully reformulate what constitutes human life and marriage, and if it can even erase the lines that distinguish man from woman, then it can do anything.

Abortion, gay marriage, "transgenderism," feminism— these are the projects most crucial to liberalism because they give godlike powers to the individual. They may be the most profound declarations of autonomy and starkest repudiations of Natural and Divine Law human beings have ever concocted. They eat away the fabric of existence. They destroy the things that are the most real and the most necessary to establishing and maintaining a good and God-fearing culture. They aim to seize control of the very things that nobody but God can control.

All people and cultures probably reject truth to some extent or another, but ours aims to forsake it completely, as a matter of principle. With abortion, we deny the nature of human life. With the homosexual movement, we deny the nature of marriage. With the work of the transgender movement and the feminist movement, we deny the nature of sex. Taken together, this Unholy Trinity denies the nature of reality itself.

They say we're in the middle of a culture war, but

there doesn't often appear to be an actual war in this war of ours. Liberalism has raped and pillaged and plundered basically at will, with very little in the way of opposition. If there is going to be another side, a resistance, those who wish to be a part of it must understand where the central battles are being fought. "Conservatism," if it's going to finally take a serious stand to salvage our civilization before it becomes officially unsalvageable, must engage primarily on these three fronts. It has to block and drive back the assault on life, marriage, and gender. If it is going to reclaim the culture, this is where that battle will be won or lost.

2

The High Sacrament

WHY ABORTION IS LIBERALISM'S
CROWNING ACHIEVEMENT

If you find yourself teetering close to the edge of almost believing there might be some faint glimmer of truth or reason left in liberalism, just remember abortion. If ever you're feeling generous enough to assume that liberalism, while morally bankrupt, really means well in the end, simply recall abortion. Think of abortion whenever that polite part of your brain tells the gullible part of your brain to tell the reasonable part of your brain that liberalism isn't really so bad after all.

Abortion—a cancer in the bloodstream of American society; a depraved, nefarious, shameful practice; a travesty of historic proportions, and one that should be garnering an enormous amount of your attention and anger.

There is no more important national "issue" than this. Abortion unravels the fabric of society, subverts the sacred institution of the family, and turns parents into something like alligators eating their young. Many civilizations have made victims of some vast group or another, but ours is the first to turn the propagated into the prey of their propagators. It takes a depraved culture to simply kill its children, but it takes an especially sadistic one to hand the gun to the mother and say, "Here, you do it."

I have no doubt that if the Devil came to Earth in physical form and wanted to find a job, he'd certainly apply to become an abortion doctor at Planned Parenthood. That is, unless Democrats moved to elect him president first.

But if I can give the disgusting practice of abortion any credit, I'll say that at least it does the valuable service of providing us with a daily reminder of modern liberalism's true nature. Like its author, Satan, progressive doctrine often comes coiffed, hip, pleasant, wearing trendy hats, and saying dumb, popular things like "Tolerance for all" and "Love wins" and "Heteronormativity causes the otherization of non-cisgendered communities" and so on. Yet at its core lies a deep animosity toward life itself.

If you peek under liberalism's shiny veneer—the happy slogans, the catchy hashtags, the rainbow flags—you'll find the corpses of fifty million dead children, decaying, ignored, forgotten by our culture of emasculated narcissists. What you see there, so gruesome and infuriating at the very rotting heart of modern liberalism, is an indictment of our entire society.

The legalization and cultural acceptance of mass infanticide is, to this day, liberalism's crowning achievement. The killing of children is considered even holier and more sacred to its disciples than gay marriage or genital mutilation. It is now the rock and foundation of the movement, and the centerpiece of its cultural agenda. Like the primitive pagan cultures that preceded it, liberal culture looks upon the sacred rite of child sacrifice with a deep reverence. Liberals venerate it for the same reason Catholics venerate the Eucharist and Muslims the Koran—because it is the centerpiece of their worship, the core, the soul of the thing.

A progressive can perhaps deviate from the script on gun rights or economic concerns, but on abortion he must be an extremist, or he will be disowned. We should emphasize that all "pro-choice" advocacy is, inherently, extremism. It is impossible to be moderately in favor of abortion, just as it is impossible to be moderately opposed to it. Seeking a middle ground on abortion is like searching for a middle ground on child rape. It doesn't exist, and those who wish to find it will inevitably end up in favor, and those in favor of murderous atrocities are always *extremely* in favor of murderous atrocities.

Whether you know it or not, your acceptance—however moderate—of a deep and depraved evil will send you barreling into a darkness that will utterly distort your moral compass. What you thought was a celebration of your own precious life will lead you to bow at the altar of the Culture of Death.

Your conscience is not a lunch tray, with all of the different components neatly separated into their own compartments. Your conscience is more like a bucket, and everything you dump into it will mingle and mix with everything else. The point is, if you pour an acceptance of child murder into your bucket, it will poison everything, and soon even the good parts will be colored and tainted by your tacit endorsement of violence against the innocent. It changes you, and how you see the world. This *will* happen. There is no way around it. Anyone who celebrates or endorses abortion but then pretends to recoil at any other form of murder is lying. They are lying to themselves, and to you.

AN ALL-OR-NOTHING PROPOSITION

It can be said that if liberalism were right about abortion, it would be right about everything else. If it were right about abortion, the value of human life would be relative to how desirable that life is to those around it. And if human life is relative, then the ideas at the root of our country—inalienable rights and dignities endowed by a Creator, yadda yadda, et cetera—can't be objectively true. God Himself cannot be true.

If we can determine the worthiness of human life, then we are gods, and truth is whatever we say it is. For this reason, liberalism has long established abortion as the primary platform for its campaign against truth, God, and reason. Abortion, as we will see, sets the stage for every other cultural battle.

MORE THAN A SIDESHOW

Many on the right still don't understand this central fact. Conservatives often pretend they can sufficiently debunk liberal ideology without addressing its holiest sacrament. They treat abortion like a sideshow, a topic of moderate importance—one that can be debated but is better avoided.

A lot of these people—those in the ever-growing Irrelevant Wuss Faction (IWF) of the conservative camp—insist that matters of human life, family, sex, and marriage are merely "social issues," which should be considered less essential than the more serious topics of debt and spending.

Indeed, according to the IWF, one can be soft on the technical matter of the fate of human civilization but still be considered "conservative" so long as he likes guns, hates taxes, and listens to country music. There's nothing wrong with liking guns, hating taxes, and listening to country—unless it's Luke Bryan we're talking about—but we are not defined by our degree of affection for these things. And it's certainly impossible to launch any coherent defense of economic or Second Amendment freedoms if you haven't first explained why we have the right to exist in the first place.

All liberties spring from our inherent worthiness as human beings. If you're willing to concede that such worthiness is conditional, or not worth arguing about, then you're willing to concede that all of our liberties are similarly frivolous and debatable.

This is what makes abortion a defining issue. It gets right down to the fundamentals of who you are and what you believe. It plants you either firmly on the side of objective truth and human dignity or firmly against it. Everything—whatever else you believe—will grow from this root. This is the epicenter of America's vast ideological divide and the Father of the Left's Unholy Trinity.

A MODERN SLAVERY

Every era seems to have its own collection of creeps insisting that an unfortunate segment of the human race isn't quite as human as the others. In this era we call them "pro-choicers"; in previous eras they were Nazis or slave owners.

The comparison of slave owners to abortion advocates is particularly apt, since both peculiar American institutions defy the universal moral principle that all human beings should be treated like human beings. Really, all of human history can be divided down this line. Those who say "Humans should be treated as humans because they are human" on one side, and those who say "Chill, bro, not so fast" on the other. Whether the member of the latter group is a feminist, a concentration camp guard, a slave trader, or Genghis Khan is only a matter of semantics. The evil is the same. The bloodshed is inevitable.

Moreover, both slave owners and abortion enthusiasts share the distinction of having had their views officially sanctioned by the Supreme Court. In *Dred Scott*, the Robed Ones decided that slaves weren't people, that because they weren't people they were property, and that because they were non-people property, they would be granted no constitutional protections. In *Roe*, a different set of Robed Ones came to the same conclusion, but this time applied it to babies. They were wrong each time, and it should be noted that blacks made out poorly in both cases. There have been over sixteen million black children killed by abortion since *Roe*. If not for abortion, the black population would be significantly larger than it is today. If liberals really want to form a diverse nation where minorities are no longer in the minority, they should probably stop encouraging those minorities to extinguish themselves.

Abortion has accomplished what the most passionate racists of yesteryear could have only dreamed. And if you investigate the arguments those racists made to justify their own favorite institution, you'll find they sound an awful lot like the arguments made by abortion enthusiasts of today. Just go right down the list:

> **Appeal to privacy:** "Who are you to tell someone what to do with their own property/body?"
>
> **Appeal to the superseding right:** "My property/body rights come before the rights of a slave/fetus."
>
> **Appeal to inevitability:** "Slavery/abortion has been around for thousands of years; it's never going to go away. We might as well have a safe and legal system in place for it."
>
> **Appeal to pseudoscience:** "Slaves/fetuses aren't really people. They aren't like us. Look at them—they're

physically different. Therefore, we are human and they are not."

Appeal to socioeconomic concerns: "If slavery/abortion ends, most of these slaves/babies will end up on the street without a job."

Appeal to the courts: "Slavery/abortion was vindicated by the Supreme Court. It's already been decided; there's no point in arguing it."

Appeal to faux compassion: "Slavery/abortion is in the best interest of Africans/babies. The world can be a cruel place. It's best to protect them from it by keeping them enslaved/killing them."

Appeal to the Bible: "Slavery/abortion isn't specifically condemned in the Bible. If it's wrong, Jesus would have specifically said so."

Slavery is, it turns out, the great-great-great-great-grandfather of abortion.

But the family resemblance is only partial. Slavery, whether in America or anywhere else in the world, subjugated only a select sample of the human species. It animalized and oppressed members of a certain race or ethnicity or nationality or social class. It didn't dehumanize humanity itself but particular sections of it. This, of course, doesn't lessen the sheer brutality and horror of slavery; it just perhaps sheds some light on the paradoxical fact that slaveholding societies still contributed enormously to the general enlightenment of mankind. They often demonstrated a profound understanding of human dignity and Natural Law, our Founding Fathers being a prime example.

Modern Americans, liberals particularly, often remark on the fact that our founders fought so valiantly for human rights yet apparently lacked the wisdom to see how these concepts should apply to Africans. Thomas Jefferson wrote one of the most insightful and inspiring political documents of all time, the Declaration of Independence, but evidently couldn't see how the notion of "independence" ought to apply to his own slaves.

To his credit, Jefferson forcefully opposed slavery in the abstract, although he practiced it personally, even making one slave his concubine. This was an extraordinary sin, obviously, yet not a sin that prevented him from seeing the deeper truths outside of slavery. He was not alone here. Indeed, scores of the greatest, wisest, most virtuous thinkers and philosophers of all time—Aristotle, Plato, Augustine, and Aquinas among them—either viewed slavery as in keeping with the natural order or thought it at least inevitable.

How could men so good and so intelligent have been so wrong about slavery? Well, not to oversimplify the issue, but nobody is perfect. More crucially, however, it appears these ancient people didn't need to dismantle their entire moral framework to justify, rationalize, or ignore the atrocity of slavery.

CATACLYSMIC REPERCUSSIONS

Abortion, on the other hand, is a more jealous evil. It will not allow its proponents to otherwise maintain their moral reasoning. While slavery existed as an accepted practice around the globe for thousands of years, abortion has been a legal institution in the United States for less than fifty. Legalized abortion has been around the longest in places like Sweden and Denmark, and even there it's barely eighty years old. Yet in this short time, especially in Western culture, there has been a complete moral collapse. The Judeo-Christian values that formed and shaped our civilization have been almost entirely erased—a process that directly correlates with the legalization of abortion. For millennia, societies have been able to maintain a sense of goodness and virtue despite their acceptance of various evils, but that is no longer the case. In the West, we have renounced virtue entirely, not just in practice but in theory.

Over the decades, we have shown ourselves quite adept at innovating new technologies and consumer goods, but in the realm of morality and spirituality, there has been a constant, precipitous decline. Our culture produces genius inventors and salesmen, but idiot philosophers and moral teachers. There is a gaping abyss where our soul should be, and I believe abortion lies at the center of it all, as both a cause and an effect.

I think part of the reason why our moral senses cannot survive if we accept abortion, even though they did survive humanity's acceptance of slavery and other sins, is that abortion doesn't debase certain people, but all people. It says that we—everyone—are parasitic and expendable throughout our earliest, most innocent, and vulnerable stages. In a sense, it deprives humanity of its humanity.

AN UNEQUAL IMPACT

I don't mean to suggest that abortion victimizes all people equally. Yes, our acceptance of the practice robs the dignity from all of mankind, yet it has had a disproportionate impact on some communities. Because of abortion, being conceived black in this country is a dangerous proposition. As I mentioned, sixteen million unborn black children have been slaughtered in the past four decades. African-Americans make up only 13 percent of the population, but they account for almost 40 percent of all abortions. Abortion doctors—whether by surgery or prescription—kill more black people in a week than the Ku Klux Klan has in the past century. Hundreds of black lives are ended by abortion every single day in the United States. Try to reflect on this statistic: abortion kills more black people than heart disease, cancer, strokes, accidents, diabetes, homicide, and respiratory illness—combined. Throw cops in there, too, and it's still not close.

Black people aren't just suffering individualized dehumanization and extermination at the hands of the infanticide industry; they are being fundamentally weakened as a race, as a people, and as a culture by the mass slaughter of the younger generations.

At the bottom of every social ill that afflicts any group, you will find the deterioration of the family unit. From poor and black to rich and white to every combination in between in America, we are all at some stage of collective self-destruction because we have all allowed our foundation—the nuclear family—to decay. But for black Americans the situation is far worse, the disease more advanced, and the prognosis much bleaker.

Maybe you've heard the numbers. Some 70 percent of black kids are born out of wedlock. A full 50 percent or more grow up in fatherless homes, and for black children in the inner city, that number is close to 90 percent. I'm no anthropologist, but I think it's safe to say that no group in human history has seen its family structure plummet into such deep disarray. This is one of humanity's greatest tragedies, and it is greeted mostly with silence.

The acceptance and practice of abortion both fuels and is fueled by the destruction of the family unit. The two feed each other, like a two-headed beast that eats itself from both ends. Because of abortion, there are fewer black men and women available to make a difference. Fewer around to raise families. Fewer in existence to right the wrongs and steer the ship. Because of abortion, there is more death and discord, more grief, more loss. Because of abortion, the idea that black lives don't matter settles into the minds of many, especially the black mothers who are so much more likely to decide to have their own children exterminated.

Therefore, if we celebrate abortion, we celebrate the self-destruction of African-Americans, and the dehumanization of all people. We might limply suggest that upon our physical passage through the birth canal, we magically inherit the value and dignity of human life. But this is the rationale of people not yet able to directly confront the hideousness of their own beliefs. If you believe that you began life as an empty, arbitrary blob of matter, you must believe, even if you will not face it, that you are still nothing more than an arbitrary blob—if perhaps more formed and functional. Our dignity and worth are either innate or they are not. And if they are not, then in the end, we are left with nothing but nihilism and materialism.

Abortion degrades and hollows out everyone. It robs children of their lives, mothers of their children, and society of its purpose for existing in the first place. And from the people who accept it, abortion demands the abandonment of belief in the dignity of man. It requires its defenders to become, as C. S. Lewis said, men without chests.

With this in mind, it might seem odd that liberals would go to such lengths to preserve "abortion rights" when that preservation comes at such an intellectual and spiritual cost. But this is precisely the point. Abortion is central to liberalism exactly because it is so devastating to Natural Law. It is crucial to their agenda; you might say that in some ways it *is* their agenda.

For progressives, abortion establishes and reinforces, at the beginning, their three primary tenets.

MAKING ALL THINGS RELATIVE

First, relativism. Progressivism is an ideology not of progress but of relativism. Indeed, it certainly can't be both; relativism makes progress impossible. Progress requires fixed points and measurable distances. To go from one place to another, you need to have a start, an end, and solid ground along the way. With relativism, though, the whole world moves as you do. The realities and definitions of things change with your opinions, and your opinions with your desires, and your desires with your mood. A country steeped in relativism cannot possibly make progress north or south, east or west, because all of our compasses are aligned not with Earth's magnetic field but with our individual emotional states.

We become like a group of maniacs trying to give an injured man directions to the hospital. Some of us tell him to turn left and drive for two miles, others say to go right for eight, others say to go straight, others say he should sprout wings and fly to the moon, others deny that there is a hospital, others have no idea but randomly take sides in the debate anyway. Finally, the guy collapses and dies and we go back to running in circles, shouting at each other, each of us sure of our correctness because in our worlds there can be no such thing as "incorrect."

It is moral and intellectual anarchy. We argue over the truth while simultaneously denying that it exists. Relativism rips out humanity's heart, soul, and brain, and leaves the shell floating there in the void, entirely susceptible to the ideological trends of the day.

Western civilization, up until recently, had been grounded in the confidence of absolute truth, which was born of belief in an absolute God. Liberalism's great project, then, is to abolish the absolutes and create a world of grays. There is no tool more effective in this effort than abortion.

It relativizes the deepest and previously most concrete moral concepts by suggesting that murder itself can be justified if committed by a mother against her child.

It's probably worthwhile to pause here for a moment and reflect on the fact that abortion advocates have largely stopped arguing that the child is not human. This is still an argument in the arsenal, but it's no longer primary. In fact, often they will admit that the child is human, or at least that it could be, yet propose that killing it can be permissible if that's what the child's mother desires. They would obviously never use the word *murder*, but if they aren't bothering to argue that the "fetus" isn't human, then they are, in effect, admitting that the act is murder.

Last year, an online campaign called "Shout Your Abortion" took social media by storm. Women were encouraged to log on to their Twitter and Facebook accounts and, in effect, brag about their abortions. Hundreds of feminists happily took part in this celebration of infanticide, unapologetically "shouting" about their wonderful abortion experiences. Many offered their reasons for having one, but few cited the biological, ethical, or legal standing of the "fetus" as a reason. Most simply asserted that they had an abortion because it was the right thing for them at the time.

For abortion proponents to offer any other justification would be to leave the door open for, if not legal, then moral parameters on the practice. If abortion is permissible because the baby is not a person, then it stands to reason that if we can scientifically prove that the baby is a person, abortion would no longer be acceptable. Abortion advocates cannot allow for even the possibility of restrictions or moral implications. So they have largely settled on a more encompassing rationalization: abortion is good because that's what the woman wants. Period.

A little while ago, a pro-life student at the University of North Georgia wrote to tell me about a pro-choice demonstration that had been staged on her campus a few days before. She said the pro-abortion group had printed out flyers with the phrase "I support abortion rights because . . . ," and liberals were invited to come and fill out their own personal reasons. The student sent me a picture of what one young pro-choice woman had written: "I support abortion rights because my vagina is too pretty to let a fetus crawl out of it."

In other words, I support abortion because I want to have abortions. My reasons for wanting one are not relevant. If I must give you a reason, I'll choose the vilest and most flippant one imaginable, just to make the message exceedingly clear. This is about what I want. And abortion is right because I want it.

In March of 2016, an article was published on Fusion .net with the headline "I Had an Abortion and It Was a Totally Joyful Experience." The column was accompanied by a giant image of a smiley face and champagne emojis. The author, Kristen Brown, detailed her own abortion tale, but noticeably did not offer a thesis on the personhood of the child. She skipped right over that part and spent most of the article explaining how her abortion made her life so much better.

"The ability to choose for myself when and if I want children was empowering—it affirmed for me that I am in control of how I choose to live my life," she wrote. Whether the "fetus" was living or not living, human or not human, is irrelevant. It was her choice. It was her life. And that's all that needs to be said.

This is an incredibly significant development on the pro-abortion side. After all, many civilizations have, as we've discussed, legalized the oppression, abuse, and destruction of certain sorts of human beings, but generally the murderers have at least had the decency to offer the rationale that the beings aren't human. They recognized Natural Law and felt the need to work around it. That certainly doesn't excuse anything, but it shows that few societies until modern times have explicitly legalized murder. Some did legalize the killing or subjugation of humans on the basis that the humans weren't humans. Some did legalize murder and call it something else. It was still murder, but they were compelled to rationalize it. The rationalizations were faulty, of course, but it is significant that they were made, that these societies were working around Natural Law rather than just rejecting it outright.

Rarely has a civilization looked upon the death and bloodshed it has wrought, shrugged its shoulders, and said, "Well, this is what we wanted, so it's OK." Rarely have the murderers said, "Yes, these are people, we have killed them, and so what?"

But with abortion it seems we have reached that virtually unprecedented point in history. In fact, undercover footage captured by the Center for Medical Progress in 2014 revealed abortionists and abortion industry insiders saying exactly that. In one video documenting a panel discussion among abortionists at an abortion industry conference in San Francisco, a woman tells the crowd, "Let's just give [pro-life activists] all the violence, it's a person, it's killing. Let's just give them all that. And then the more compelling question is, 'So, why is this the most important thing I could do with my life?'"

This isn't a Natural Law work-around. This is a total rejection of morality as we know it. This is relativism at its darkest and most extreme.

Of course, the pro-aborts will still try to find hairs to

split, insisting that the unborn human, though it might be made of human tissue, isn't a person. Here, once more, the matter is relative. Abortion advocates will often say that a baby is a person if the mother thinks it is or wants it to be, but not if she doesn't. Melissa Harris-Perry, a former host on MSNBC, told her audience in 2013 that the woman's "feelings" are the real marker for when life begins. "When does life begin? I submit the answer depends an awful lot on the feeling of the parents. A powerful feeling—but not science. The problem is that many of our policymakers want to base sweeping laws on those feelings."

By this line of reasoning, personhood itself is relative and contingent upon "feelings." She, and many liberals just like her, proudly deny that science has any bearing on the abortion question at all. Personhood is relative, they insist. We'll deal more with that line of reasoning in the next chapter.

MAKING SEX SELFISH

Second, abortion establishes and reinforces the liberal narrative about sex. There have been, throughout history, two competing claims about human sexuality. One says that sex is, first and foremost, a recreational activity to be enjoyed between two adults (or five adults, or an adult and a farm animal, or whatever other combination).

In this view, the sexual act is self-focused. I am concerned with what I can take from my partner, what she can give me.

Sex becomes analogous to something like playing a video game. I may be playing with someone because playing by myself gets boring after a while, but I'm certainly playing for my own sake. If the other person derives enjoyment out of it, good for them, but that's not my primary concern. And, obviously, I am not pursuing anything nobler or holier than mere enjoyment.

That gives rise to the second claim. Christians, and adherents to other theistic faiths, propose that sex is quite a bit more consequential and profound than video games. We are engaging with another human being on the most intimate level possible, and our emotions, our desires, our spirits are tangled up in the act. And from that act—this is what sets it apart from all other activities—a whole new human life can be formed. Video games are getting more advanced these days, but as far as I'm aware they still haven't developed one with that feature.

Sex is an enjoyable activity, but enjoyment is not the final end of the act. It is not the purpose. The purpose is to give yourself to another, to express your love and devotion to your spouse, to deepen and strengthen the marital bond. And if we are of the right age and right health, and if we give ourselves totally, without reserving anything or putting any artificial barriers between us, there is always the possibility that the unitive sexual act becomes, at the same time, a procreative act. Both the unitive and procreative aspects of sex are essential. They are dimensions of the whole, and if we destroy one, we deny the other.

This notion of love and sex was beautifully illustrated in the Song of Songs:

> My lover speaks; he says to me, "Arise, my beloved, my dove, my beautiful one, and come! O my dove in the clefts of the rock, in the secret recesses of the cliff, let me see you, let me hear your voice, for your voice is sweet, and you are lovely." My lover belongs to me and I to him. He says to me: "Set me as a seal on your heart, as a seal on your arm; for stern as death is love, relentless as the nether-world is devotion; its flames are a blazing fire. Deep waters cannot quench love, nor floods sweep it away."

For comparison's sake, the modern, progressive idea of love and sex was succinctly captured by Beyoncé in her 2013 hit "Drunk in Love":

> Park it in my lot, 7-Eleven,
> I'm rubbing on it, rub-rubbing, if you scared, call
> that reverend.

Aside from being nonsensical, this, and virtually any other pop song recorded since about 1958, sums up the progressive sexual philosophy. Let me have fun. Let me get mine. Or, as the modern Shakespeare puts it, "Park it in my lot, 7-Eleven."

Abortion is needed to maintain this idea of sex. If sex is supposed to be a frivolous, self-centered pursuit of enjoyable physical sensations, then babies must be seen as "accidents." Unintentional and unwelcomed by-products of an encounter that had nothing to do with them.

But this is like planting a seed in the ground and calling it a mistake when a tree begins to sprout, claiming that you thought the soil was infertile. You may have believed this, but still the seed is doing exactly what seeds are supposed to do, and you did exactly what a person is supposed to do if they want to make a tree grow. You may be a fool, but this was no accident.

Next, you cut down the sapling and toss it in the fire, and then you continue to plant seeds. Each time, you cry that all of these damned trees keep shooting out of the ground. When someone comes and tells you to stop planting until you're ready to deal with a forest, you weep and accuse the person of being cruel and judgmental simply because she's articulating the basic rules of botany.

Of course, this metaphor fails for one reason: everyone agrees that you shouldn't kill baby trees for no reason. No such consensus exists when it comes to baby people.

When a culture accepts the notion that babies are accidental by-products of intercourse—usurpers intruding on a couple's sexual recreation—we end up with an idea of sex that is not only selfish, but fearful.

This is where our current obsession with "safe sex" originates. We grind it into our kids' heads from a young age, especially in public school health classes, and it fosters in them a pessimistic, reductionist view of human sexuality. Today, kids never hear anything positive about sex because the positive aspects have been recast as negatives.

Positive: sex creates human beings. This is a great good, but it isn't a good that humans should pursue until they are married and prepared to care for the life they've formed.

Positive: sex is an expression of love. This is the primary thing that separates human sex from sex between beasts. It is a profound good.

These are the two most beautiful things about sex, but we have decided to teach our children that they can and should begin "exploring their sexuality" one or two decades before they'll be able to truly embrace every magnificent dimension of it. So for the next ten or fifteen years, they will learn to see the two greatest things about sex as among the worst. Unsurprisingly, this attitude will often stay with them, permanently.

Not to wander too far off the subject, but this is why the abstinence-before-marriage plan is better. It paints an affirmative and uplifting picture. It says, "This is something so good and so important and so joyful that you should leave it be until you grow up and find one special person to share it with."

The "safe sex" model, however, tells a paranoid story. It says, "This is something so frivolous and so joyless that you can do it with whomever, for whatever reason, even if just to alleviate boredom. By the way, though it is just a recreational activity, like Parcheesi or air hockey, it can also lead to broken hearts, chlamydia, pregnancy, and AIDS. So, in that sense, it's a little different from a board game. Hey, let's look at some super-magnified images of genital warts!"

And, somehow, that version gets to pretend it's the "positive" and "encouraging" one. The only comfort it offers is that sex can be fun, but, in lieu of introducing morality, responsibility, and delayed gratification into the conversation, it has to guide the child's behavior by warning them of the dangers of pubic lice and teenage pregnancy.

Abortion rights are necessary for progressives because they solidify this version of sex in the public conscience.

MAKING HUMANS GOD

Third, abortion elevates human beings above God. This is the ultimate goal of what we call progressivism. As we've seen, progressivism is just the modern term for the movement that started back before the beginning of time, when Satan turned away from God and said, "I will not serve." That's what all of this is. That's what this book is about. That's what our "culture war" is being fought over: Will we serve ourselves or God?

There probably isn't anything that answers that question more definitively than abortion. When God hands us a life and we say no and throw it aside, we are saying no to God Himself. We are saying that the power to grant life or death ought to reside with us. We are saying that we will not serve God's will, even if it means murdering our own young.

MANHOOD AND WOMANHOOD DESTROYED

And, in the process of rejecting God's will, we reject ourselves. This is one of the great tragedies of abortion: it destroys not only lives but motherhood itself, womanhood itself. Manhood itself. Or it may be more accurate to say that liberalism has set out to conquer and destroy these things, and abortion is just a vehicle—the most effective vehicle—to that end.

However you put it, it's clear that you cannot support abortion without sacrificing your femininity and masculinity. Feminine women—real women—are compassionate, merciful, and nurturing. That is the beautiful gift they give to their families, and to society. Men, for our part, give justice, protection, and moral leadership. Now, that isn't to say men can't be merciful and compassionate and women just and protective, but men by their nature are especially inclined and equipped to provide justice, protection, and moral leadership, and women compassion, mercy, and nurturance.

Families can only properly function when there is a man and a woman working together, providing that careful balance of justice and mercy, compassion and protection, leadership and nurturance. But men and women in our country have begun to lose these traits, and I believe our culture's acceptance and advocacy of abortion is a catalyst for this regression.

It is, after all, impossible for a woman to be a fountain of feminine grace and mercy while condoning the murder of children. A man, likewise, must be vacated of his instinct and passion for justice, his urge to protect the innocent, and his desire to provide moral leadership if he is going to be an effective apologist for infanticide. Both are emptied of what makes them distinct and important, creating the sort of hollow, androgynous society we currently see developing around us.

As a side note, any man who has gone shopping for pants recently is deeply aware of our collective slide into androgyny. I couldn't help but shake my head at the state of modern masculinity recently as I stumbled flabbergasted through the department stores in my local mall, unable to tell if I was in the men's section or the women's section or the toddlers' section or the section where weirdos buy clothes for their cats and poodles. At one point, I stood in horror and stared at a rack full of men's camo denim spandex pants. It looked like something a twelve-year-old girl would wear to go paintballing, but this is what men wear nowadays, apparently.

This may not be the most serious symptom of the underlying problem, but there has been, in our shopping malls and far beyond, a breakdown in society's understanding of what men and women are supposed to be doing, what role they ought to be playing, and what they ought to be providing in their families and their communities. Abortion isn't the sole cause of this—you might say it's as much an effect as a cause—but it's all tied together, either way.

This is to say nothing of what the act of abortion does to the women who participate. As angry as I am about the practice, I always make sure to remember that post-abortive women are victims, too. Clinics often target the young, the poor, and the scared, feeding on their fear and desperation, whispering to them like the snake in the

Garden of Eden, promising that if they only refuse the gift they've been given, everything will be OK. These clinics spread the most insidious and most popular deception in modern culture: that women can be "empowered" precisely by rejecting their greatest power. That by ripping the fruit from their womb, violently denying the beautiful truth of motherhood, they can be made whole again.

This is not true. The death of a child can never ultimately benefit his mother. And she *is* his mother, whether he's dead or alive. The abortion factories tell women they can somehow undo the past and return to their days of not being a mother, but no such option is actually available. Once the child is conceived, motherhood has occurred.

If she aborts the baby, she will simply become the mother of a dead child. This is a tragedy in and of itself, and one that ought to fill us with incredible compassion and pity for the women who are taken in by the lie only to be left abandoned, alone, confused, and guilt-ridden, mourning a life they were told never existed.

This is abortion. It breeds regret, emptiness, and shame. It deprives women of the love and joy of motherhood. It deprives children of their lives. It deprives the world of the hope and promise every new life brings to this Earth. It leaves a giant hole, a chasm, a silence where these millions of human beings were supposed to be.

It is a tragedy on a cosmic scale.

Abortion is meant to make us gods. But, in the end, like the Father of Lies, it reduces us to nothingness.

3

The Autonomy Myth

WHY A MOTHER'S BODY IS NOT
SOLELY HER OWN

Abortion is often treated, even among some pro-lifers, as a complicated and nuanced moral issue with many challenging dimensions. However, in truth it's very simple. Assessing the exact moral culpability of any participant in an abortion might be more complex, but we are not tasked, as human beings, with making that determination. All we can do is judge the rightness or wrongness of an act itself, and taking the life of an innocent child always falls rather severely on the "wrong" side of the equation. If anything at all can be considered wrong, then killing a defenseless human being must qualify. This is why, as we've established, our culture must fall back on blanket moral relativism to protect abortion. Once you let even the faintest hint of an objective moral truth seep in, you jeopardize your rationalizations for child murder.

The pro-abortion camp is in a precarious spot arguing in favor of something that seems so obviously and immediately repugnant. But they do have the enviable advantage of not being tied to one justification or another. They float untethered in a morally incoherent fog. They can pick up an argument and drop it just as quickly. It doesn't matter. Only truth needs to be consistent. Lies can contradict themselves all day long.

For this reason, debating a progressive can feel a bit like wrestling a giant mutant slug. It isn't particularly skilled, but it is slimy. You think you have it nailed down with one move, but next thing you know it's slithering on top of you and eating your face, or doing whatever giant gastropods do. Take down one point and it slides on to the next.

The point is, it can be difficult to win an argument with a "pro-choicer" because one argument so quickly turns into several: she starts a conversation about rape and incest, or insists that babies aren't people, or shouts vapid slogans about a woman's "right to choose."

Let's respond to each of these, one at a time:

Argument: What about rape?

I have to address this point not because it's compelling or valid, but because it's inevitable. If you argue with a liberal about abortion for more than twelve seconds, they are guaranteed to pull the rape card. Think of this as a version of Godwin's Law, that famous principle that says all debates on the internet will devolve until someone brings up Hitler.

Admittedly I've already brought up Hitler, which wasn't entirely fair to Hitler. The Nazis killed some ten or eleven million when they were in power. The abortion industry, on the other hand, kills about forty million *a year*. And it's been going strong for half a century. You do the math.

Rape is obviously a serious matter, but it has no actual bearing on the abortion question. Aside from the fact that abortions because of rape are exceedingly rare (they account for about 1 percent of all abortions), the larger point is that the murder of a human being can't be justified by the actions of a third party. Either a "fetus" is a human with a right to live and be protected by the law, or it isn't. If it is, the manner of its conception is not relevant. If it isn't, the manner of its conception is still not relevant.

Liberals bring rape into the abortion debate as a means of obfuscation. I prefer not to play that game, so let's move on.

Argument: So never mind how it was conceived. A baby isn't a person/human—it's just a lump of cells.

Lump: a compact mass of a substance.

Cell: the smallest structural and functional unit of an organism.

Yes, babies are "lumps of cells," just as you are. Actually, if you look anything like the average Walmart shopper, you're probably quite a bit lumpier than the average "fetus." Trying to disqualify a human from the human race on the grounds that it is a compact substance composed of cells is like disqualifying a car from the classification of "automobile" because you have decided it is a metallic structure with wheels and an engine. And how could it be both?

But most moderately sophisticated liberals (a small sample group, to be sure) will not try to seriously pretend that an unborn baby is categorically unhuman. The fact that it is human is not remotely debatable. We know that "fetus," which simply means "offspring," is not a species but a stage of human development. It seems rather impossible that a thing could be in a stage of human development yet not be human. It seems impossible that a thing could be one species and then become another.

So we know that it is human, but is it alive? Well, if it isn't alive, what is it? Dead? The dictionary provides two definitions for "life": (1) "the condition that distinguishes animals and plants from inorganic matter, including the capacity for growth, reproduction, functional activity, and continual change preceding death," and (2) "the existence of an individual human being or animal."

An unborn human is organic, it is growing, it is functioning, it is changing, and it does exist. By any measure, it lives. It's certainly closer to a living human than it is to a rock or a computer or a roll of paper towels. Is there a state of existence between paper towel and human? If so, science has vastly failed us, because all any scientist has ever said since the beginning of time is that a thing is either living organic matter or it is not. To my knowledge, there is no such thing as "living-ish."

An unborn child is not a sperm or an egg. The "fetus" is not waiting for some other ingredient to be added to it. It has, at the moment of conception, all that it needs to grow and develop. It is a *being*—a genetically distinct individual with its own DNA, its own blood type, its own chromosomes. Granted, it has to exist for a while in its mother's womb in order for it to mature and reach whatever state of development the modern liberal subjectively decides it must reach, but just because it requires a certain environment and must have access to certain nutrients doesn't change the fact that it's human. You and I require that too.

Are you less human because you need to be on Earth breathing oxygen, drinking water, discharging your bowels, eating, and sleeping? Your life depends on your always having access to a very specific environment and very specific nutrients. You are a fragile little thing whose continued existence demands that many factors come together at all times.

Does that mean you're not quite as human as someone who requires less sleep, or who eats less, or who is generally stronger and more capable of withstanding harsh environments?

If our humanity depends on our development and our ability to survive without vital nutrients, then it stands to reason that this game of assigning degrees of humanness based on strength, physical maturity, and lack of dependency should continue beyond birth. LeBron James is more physically advanced than you; therefore, he is more human. A child with cerebral palsy is less advanced, and therefore less human. This is quite the scary world we're constructing. One where the disabled can be discarded and NBA stars can be gods.

Come to think of it, that pretty well describes our culture right now.

Thank you, liberalism.

Now, what about personhood? Can a thing be alive and human but not an actual person? Liberals say so, but you'll notice they never actually define the term *person*. This is their game with virtually every topic: attack the old definition, refuse to offer a new one.

They'll say that the unborn child from conception

lacks the limbs, organs, and other physical features necessary to be considered a person. But does this mean that once it attains those necessary markers, it can be afforded the rights of all other people? Not according to the liberal. Babies at twenty weeks certainly look an awful lot like people, yet liberals reject twenty-week abortion bans. The "lump of cells" argument is based on the fact that humans do not look much like humans early on, but they don't generally follow their own logic once the human begins to develop more recognizable physical features.

If they did, they would oppose most abortions after the first trimester. Likewise, they would support abortions of humans of any age who are born missing organs or limbs or who suffer other abnormalities. If personhood is to be determined by merely resembling other people, then many people are not people, or else they are less people-y than most people. How does this work exactly? Liberalism can't explain.

Some people think that a baby is expendable before "viability," but the whole idea of viability is ridiculously vague. Never mind the fact that describing humans as "viable" or "nonviable" makes them sound like robots or science experiments. A significant percentage of babies born at twenty-three weeks, or sometimes even earlier, are "viable," in the sense that they can survive outside the womb. But that doesn't mean you can release them into the wild, leave them to their own devices, and expect them to be fine. Babies born that early require intense, constant medical attention from a team of health-care professionals. They are "viable" as long as very strict conditions are met. The same is true of newborn infants. Come to think of it, I've met plenty of twenty-five-year-olds who can't function independent of their parents' supervision and financial support. Perhaps we should move the age of viability to thirty-five.

The fact of the matter is this: either a living human is a person regardless of physical features and development and medical needs, or we should petition the government to turn the murder of midgets and the severely handicapped and deadbeat college graduates into a misdemeanor offense. Personhood is either an absolute state, or it is acquired in degrees. Personhood is either contained in the essence and nature of a human being, or it is contained in the human's physical proximity and likeness and comparable functionality to other humans. If the latter, then there is not a single coherent reason why the acquisition of personhood automatically stops at birth for all people.

But let's take a step back. Liberals are wrong when they say that unborn children aren't people, but let's engage in our own thought experiment and suppose, for a moment, that they're right. Suppose we live in Abortion Candy Land, where unborn children become people only upon emerging from the birth canal.

What of the millions of potential people populating the wombs of the world? Are they worthless? If liberals were right about the non-personhood of "fetuses," would they consequently be right about the moral legitimacy of abortion?

Nope. Still wrong.

Even in their version of things, unborn children would be, if not people, then the most valuable non-people resources on the face of the earth. They would be entities still vastly more important and precious than any endangered spotted owl or dolphin or any gold bar or diamond. They would still deserve our love, care, and protection. They wouldn't be people, but they would be worth the equivalent of one.

In this fantasy, the destruction of a fetus would be kind of like someone tearing up your winning five-hundred-million-dollar lottery ticket. Sure, the ticket itself isn't five hundred million dollars until you cash it, but it's *worth* five hundred million, isn't it? If it were destroyed, you wouldn't react like someone who'd lost a piece of paper with some numbers on it, but like someone who'd lost five hundred million dollars.

Similarly, if liberals are right about "fetuses," abortion is not the killing of a person, but it might as well be.

There would still be no significant distinction between killing a person and killing a human who is about to become a person.

Incredibly, liberal arguments are so bad that even if they were right, they'd still be wrong.

Argument: But women have the right to choose!

No, they don't, and neither do men for that matter. No human being possesses the absolute "right to choose" any more than he does the absolute right to walk or eat or speak. These are all human functions, but no rational person believes we have the "right" to do these things whenever and however we want. We don't have the right to walk into the Oval Office unannounced, or the right to eat human flesh, or the right to slander another person. We can walk many places, eat many things, and say many phrases, but there are restrictions. *Of course* there are restrictions.

I could list ten thousand choices that few people think we have a right to make. Start with any felony—murder, rape, burglary, larceny, fraud, etc.—and we already have dozens of areas where almost nobody is "pro-choice." It becomes therefore apparent that the "right to choose" is not absolute, despite how it's frequently presented by liberals. It means nothing. Everyone believes many choices ought to be permissible, and many other choices ought not. On the matter of choice, every human being on the planet takes, for different reasons, a conditional approach.

Some choices are OK, some are not. It depends on the what, the why, the where, and the how. Indeed, the ability to distinguish between a good choice and a bad one, especially on moral grounds, is among the primary capacities separating us from beasts and bugs.

Abortion supporters have, against all odds, achieved the unbelievable feat of convincing our society that you can't attack the slaughter of children without attacking free will itself. It makes me wonder if I could punch a liberal in the nose and, when he protests, claim that he is protesting not the fact that I used my arm to punch him, but the fact that I have arms in the first place. Clearly, he must be an anti-arm bigot.

This is the tried-and-true strategy of many who find themselves in the difficult situation of having to answer an unanswerable argument. Simply invent an argument nobody is making and answer that one instead. Liberalism cannot, when it comes down to it, debunk the rather simple and unassailable point that it's wrong to kill babies. Instead, they debunk the point that it's wrong to not be able to make choices, which is a point literally nobody has ever made.

THE ONLY ARGUMENT THAT MATTERS

But these arguments are all too easy to address. And, in any event, they seem to be more like warm-ups before we get to the only "pro-choice" rationalization that actually matters. As we've seen, what lies at the bottom of our progressive culture is a worship of the self. The self has been elevated above God—it has replaced Him completely—and therefore nothing and no one may make a claim on the self that supersedes its own desires. Depending on the issue, our culture has different ways of dressing up this principle. With abortion, they call it "bodily autonomy."

Liberals claim that a woman's body is autonomous— self-governed, independent—and that an unborn baby, whether human or not, has no right to his mother's body. Already, there seems to be a pretty serious logical problem with the self claiming ownership over itself. In order for one thing to own another, the owner must exist outside of, and apart from, the owned. All things that exist came into existence because of something else, so how can anything be called truly autonomous?

If there is a God, then we all originate by His hand, and certainly nobody can be considered completely sovereign. But if there is no God, then we are the result of meaningless and mechanical natural processes, and the notion of "autonomy" is even more absurd. How can one pointless accident be autonomous or independent of another? In this version of things, the only sovereign thing is nature itself, and to interfere with the natural process would be the only true moral crime. This, again, would make abortion the worst sin. Perhaps even the only sin.

Bodily autonomy has been a popular defense of abortion ever since Judith Jarvis Thomson proposed the idea with a famous thought experiment in her 1971 essay "A Defense of Abortion." This constitutes the best argument anyone has ever made for abortion, and in recent years, liberals have abandoned most of their other talking points in favor of repeating the bodily autonomy canard over and over again.

Thomson's analogy goes like this:

> You wake up in the morning and find yourself back to back in bed with an unconscious violinist. A famous unconscious violinist. He has been found to have a fatal kidney ailment, and the Society of Music Lovers has canvassed all the available medical records and found that you alone have the right blood type to help. They have therefore kidnapped you, and last night the violinist's circulatory system was plugged into yours, so that your kidneys can be used to extract poisons from his blood as well as your own. The director of the hospital now tells you, "Look, we're sorry the Society of Music Lovers did this to you—we would never have per-

mitted it if we had known. But still, they did it, and the violinist is now plugged into you. To unplug you would be to kill him. But never mind, it's only for nine months."

You see, in pregnancy, the *woman* is the slave. But rather than being forced into labor by a plantation owner, she has been brutally subjugated to labor by her baby. If you gaze into any ultrasound, you will witness not a beautiful and innocent child but a tyrant callously coercing his own mother into a life of servitude. He is, in Thomson's comparison, a stranger affixing himself through tubes and wires to the woman's internal organs—and doing so without permission, no less.

I call this the best "pro-choice" argument, but that doesn't mean it's a solid one. It's the best in the same way that, if you had to choose, you might say the guillotine is the best way to be executed. In fact, Thomson's analogy immediately brings to mind five objections:

1. The analogy assumes that the relationship between mother and child is no more significant, and carries with it no more responsibility, than the relationship between a person and some random stranger.

Absurd, obviously. If we're trying to make this hypothetical as close to pregnancy as possible, shouldn't the sick violinist at least be the woman's own child? The argument doesn't work because the fact that her child is *her child*, not some strange adult from across town, is precisely the point.

Hidden cleverly in this hypothetical is the implication that one cannot agree that an unborn child has a right to his mother's body without agreeing that *anyone* in the entire world, in any context, for any reason, at any point, for any period of time, has a right to a woman's body. One minute you're attempting to explain why a baby shouldn't be stabbed in the brain with a poison needle, and the next you're suddenly justifying rape. That's how this works, the pro-abort claims.

But just because a mother is expected to be a mother doesn't mean she's also expected to be a slave, a prostitute, or a forced organ donor to talented musical artists. Indeed, the extent of our responsibility to a person hinges in many ways on our relationship to them. Abortion fanatics would, I assume, agree that they have a special responsibility to their born children, wouldn't they? And their responsibility to them extends far beyond their responsibility to their neighbor, or their plumber, or a violinist, no matter how acclaimed.

If I go a lifetime without clothing, feeding, or changing your child, I will not face any legal repercussions. If I go two days without doing the same for mine, I could end up in prison. Why? Because they are *my* children.

Last week, my wife and I hired a babysitter so we could enjoy one meal that doesn't involve someone dumping applesauce on their lap or their sister's head. But we only hired a babysitter for our *own* kids. In fairness, I asked our sitter how much it would cost for her to watch 1.9 billion children for a couple of hours on a Friday night, but the quote was a bit out of our price range. Yet we went to the pub down the street and had our meal and drank our beer, and we still haven't heard from CPS about it.

Why is that? Because all laws everywhere in the world, and all even partially sane human beings everywhere in the world, recognize that you are particularly responsible for and to your own children. In every other instance, parents are expected, required, and forced to do things for their kids that they aren't for anyone else. Only in the case of abortion does this principle become strangely controversial.

2. The analogy leaves out an important detail: How did the violinist become ill in the first place?

Aside from cases of rape, a child is only conceived because two people intentionally committed a particular act that has, billions of times, resulted in the conception of a human life.

This violinist came down with a terrible sickness. I might feel pity for him, but I didn't cause him to be sick.

I didn't put him in this state. I had absolutely nothing to do with it. The same cannot be said when a child is conceived. To make the scenario even close to parallel, we'd have to say that the violinist is your child, *and that he is sick because you deliberately did something to make him sick.* Now, obviously in that case you wouldn't be forced to donate blood or organs, but certainly your refusal to do so would make you seem selfish and cold-blooded.

Now imagine you stabbed your son, maybe not intentionally but recklessly. Maybe you got drunk one night and decided to try your hand at knife juggling, only you failed to catch one of the knives and your infant caught it in his chest instead. Then imagine you take him to the hospital and the doctor tells you that he needs a blood transfusion quickly or he will die; luckily your blood type matches. Then imagine you say, "Nah, my body is my body. Sorry, son." You would, I assume, have this right legally. But morally, your decision would be frowned upon, to put it mildly.

Pro-aborts are fond of comparing pregnancy to organ donation—whether using this hypothetical or something similar to it—but that brings up its own question: Can you donate an organ to someone *and then take it back*? I do not think pregnancy is akin to donating your organs to your child, and even less is it akin to being forcibly hooked up to some violinist in a hospital bed. But let's say these scenarios are equal. In that case, the woman "donated" the organs to the child when she became pregnant. If she can change her mind and withdraw the offer after the fact, shouldn't we allow any organ donor to do the same? Shouldn't a man who donates a kidney be allowed to renege a few months down the line?

3. Beyond those points, the analogy is bunk because abortion is not the same as "unplugging" a person from medical equipment.

It might be quite sanitary and pleasant to refer to abortion as a woman "withdrawing support" from her child, but the procedure goes beyond this. During a "termination," the baby is actively killed. It is crushed, dismembered, or poisoned. It is actually, purposefully, intentionally killed.

In fact, even in the violinist analogy, while it would be acceptable to unplug yourself, it would not be morally or legally permissible to shoot the poor guy in the head. A person's physical reliance on you does not give you the moral (or legal, usually) right to murder them. "Pulling the plug" is precisely what an abortion *isn't*. If it were, then the baby would be delivered and left to die in the corner of the room. Of course, this *is* how some abortionists conduct business, but it's illegal. If they're caught, they go to jail. The only kind of abortion that's actually in keeping with the bodily autonomy position is precisely the kind that isn't legal or defended by the very people who assert bodily autonomy.

So to put Thomson's hypothetical in the same ball-park as abortion, we'd have to suppose that you hurt your child, then refused to give blood to save him, and then, to make your position clear, you grabbed a gun and shot him in the head.

Abortion analogies are pretty disturbing when made accurate, aren't they?

4. In any case, the analogy fails to get to the heart of the matter because it doesn't account for one crucial thing: natural order.

An unborn child is exactly where he is supposed to be. He couldn't possibly be anywhere else. This is the in-herent distinction between two strangers who have been mysteriously hooked up together on a hospital bed and a "fetus" connected to his mother inside her womb. The former represents unnatural and extraordinary mea-sures, while the latter represents something natural and ordinary. The unborn child in the womb is where nature (or God, as I call Him) intends her to be.

Unborn children are not, in any medical sense, in-truders or parasites. They are where they belong. A fish belongs in water, just as an unborn child belongs in his mother's womb. Bodily autonomy asserts, incredibly, that a baby doesn't have a right to be in his own moth-er's body, which is like saying that a bird doesn't have a right to fly, or that Earth doesn't have the right to orbit the sun, or that we don't have the right to exist in three physical dimensions. It makes no sense.

When you separate "rights" from any notion of what is not only natural but necessary to the very existence of the human race, you end up with lunacy. If "human right" means anything, it must mean, at an elemental level, that we are entitled to be what we are. The Declaration of Independence calls our rights "inalienable" and "endowed by [the] Creator." *Inalienable* means "unable to be taken away from or given away by the possessor." The only way to stop someone from expressing their inalienable right is to oppress or kill them. That is how fundamental and ingrained these rights are.

Life, at any stage, is endowed and inalienable. Therefore, to forcibly remove from a person the essential components of life and the very things that enable a person to continue living is a terrible infringement on his right to life. I cannot, through a purposeful and intentional act, deprive someone of the ability to breathe, or eat, or drink. To do so would be an attack not on his right to breathe, eat, and drink but on his right to his very life, which is necessarily sustained by breathing, eating, and drinking.

So it is with an unborn child. An unborn child is the only thing it can be, in the one place it needs to be in order to live, which is the only place it can be, and the same place that every human being who has ever lived must have been at some point. If he does not have a right to be there, where he must be, where he should be, where he is supposed to be, then truly nobody can have a right to anything.

5. All analogies aside, bodily autonomy doesn't exist anyway.

Our bodies are not autonomous.

If they were, if our bodies could never be used without our consent, why would this apply only to pregnancy and organ donations? Children, at any age, create profound demands on their parents' bodies, whether it's waking up in the middle of the night for the crying baby, working long hours to pay for their food and clothing, carrying them around when they cannot walk, staying home when you'd like to go out, or going out when you'd like to stay in. An argument for absolute bodily autonomy means that it can't be illegal, or considered immoral, for a parent to decline to do any of these things, so long as their decision was made in the name of bodily autonomy.

Take breast-feeding, for example. A child requires milk from his mother in order to survive. If she cannot or does not wish to give him that sustenance, legally she is required by law to find and pay for a substitute. She is not permitted to let her baby starve to death, or to cut to the chase and "abort" him outright. Somehow, she has to make sure he is fed, or she will go to jail on charges of neglect and murder. But even feeding the child formula is an enormous strain on the body and the bank account. You have to physically go to the store, purchase it, come home, and then wake up at all hours of the night to give it to him. He will also need feeding during the day, so you either have to be there to do it or you have to arrange and likely pay for someone else to do it for you.

All of this constitutes a claim not just on your body but on your life. As a parent, existence itself is made nonautonomous. Your body is no longer your own; your money is no longer your own; your house is no longer your own; your food, your free time—nothing is your own. Tragically, even your television is no longer your own, which means you'll find yourself cursing the name of the jerk who invented the damn thing when you're stuck on a Saturday morning watching cartoons about monkeys and talking trains instead of *SportsCenter* or *Law & Order* reruns. Everything changes. Nothing is yours anymore.

If we concede that we ought to be expected or even required to do certain things for our children, then we are invariably placing limits on our bodily autonomy. If we place limits on our bodily autonomy, then we are admitting that limits *can* be placed. If we are admitting that limits can be placed, then we must consider whether abortion falls within or outside of those limits. And here's the rub: if we contend that abortion falls within the limits of bodily autonomy, we must justify that belief *beyond simply reasserting our right to bodily autonomy.*

So we see that all justifications for abortion fall apart under scrutiny.

4

The Death Cult

WHY WE HAVE A RIGHT TO LIFE, BUT NOT A "RIGHT TO DIE"

As we've seen, mainstream culture tends toward two fundamental lies about human life: that it has no objective value, and that it is autonomous. Both of these propositions have implications far beyond the womb. If a human being manages to escape what has become the death trap of the female uterus, she will live still for a while longer in a state of vulnerability and dependence. And even when she matures past it, she will eventually return to it. But in the progressive mind, a life that relies on another life—because of age or illness or whatever reason—is subhuman, a beast, a sponge. A person who can't walk around and pay bills and post selfies to Instagram and participate in the consumer economy is less than a person. He is not functional or useful in any material sense, and worse, he is a burden. He costs money. He costs time, which is why, in a society that doesn't recognize the basic dignity of human life, it appears quite logical to start ushering this onerous parasite to the exit.

The Culture of Death is born from this mindset, and it explains not only abortion but also the modern celebration of suicide—or "euthanasia," as it's referred to in polite company.

The term *euthanasia* comes from the Greek *eu*, meaning "well" or "good," and *thanatos*, meaning "death." By even using this word, we have already redefined suicide as "good death." The death cult of liberalism looks at death as "good" when it can be considered beneficial. Abortion, you might say, is a form of euthanasia—a good death—because it "benefits" the mother by allowing her to escape responsibility, and it "benefits" society by relieving it of another burdensome unwanted child. Of course, the "good death" of abortion would seem to be not as beneficial for the child being slaughtered, but the death cultists will still insist that, somehow, it's better even for her if she is not bothered with the annoyance of having to exist. These are decisions made without the child's consent by people who so relish the idea of their own existence, and guard it so jealously, that they'd rather kill than be forced to share it.

Euthanasia is enjoying surging popularity in the United States and Europe because it can be more convincingly presented as beneficial to the victim. In Belgium, where suicide appears to be something of a national pastime, the procedure is open to everyone, including children. Horrifically, they also make it available to "patients" who are not terminally ill. All you need to do is claim chronic depression, anxiety, or a mild toothache to earn yourself a prescribed lethal injection. Strange that a country with only eleven million people is so intent on whittling the population down even further.

In 2016 it was revealed that a young woman in the Netherlands was euthanized because she suffered from emotional trauma as the result of sexual abuse. The law in that country allows "mercy killing" for anyone who experiences "unbearable suffering," even if the suffering is emotional or psychological.

Not long before that case became public, *The Economist* released a documentary about a woman in Belgium who elected to be given a lethal injection as a way to treat her chronic depression. Fortunately, she decided at the last minute not to go through with it. But it is of course deeply disturbing that such a "procedure" was ever made available to her in the first place.

All of this is deemed acceptable by Western society because, surely, if the victim *chooses* to be a victim, she is empowered. As we covered in the previous chapter, our culture proposes that choice itself—whatever the choice, and for whatever reason the choice is made—empowers. This is why liberals call themselves "pro-choice" and consider that abstract and hollow statement meaningful, as if all choices are good simply because they were made—no matter if the choice involves the destruction of life, even your own.

This is a notion that those not indoctrinated in the death cult find impossible to comprehend. But in the mind of the death cultist, it is taken for granted that the greatest expression of self-*determination* is self-*annihilation*. For this reason, euthanasia—and, really, all forms of suicide, whether "physician assisted" or otherwise—is cherished and celebrated in our society. "Cherished and celebrated" may seem a bit extreme, but consider the sick, bizarre sort of martyr status that's often granted to famous people who take their own lives. Robin Williams and Kurt Cobain were beloved in life, but their suicides turned them immediately into saints.

To make matters worse, there are few voices willing or able to dispute the case for suicide-by-doctor. The autonomous, individualistic mindset is so ingrained in us that even those who oppose the death cult find it difficult to explain *why* a person should be deprived of the right to die. Conservatives, as much as liberals, tend to build their cases from the basic premise that *my* rights are *mine*.

But if I am in fact the source of my own rights, then why *shouldn't* I kill myself (or do whatever else I want, for that matter)? We cannot debunk the liberal argument while accepting the liberal presuppositions that lead to that argument. We can try, but we will fail.

With this dearth of compelling anti-suicide arguments in mind, I'd like to outline the five primary points against euthanasia.

1. You do not have a "right to die."

We're told euthanasia is a great good because it allows a person the ability to exercise his right to die, but that phrase is utter nonsense. You can't say that death is your "right" any more than you can say it is the right of the stone that it fall to the ground after being tossed in the air. These are laws of science, unavoidable and inevitable. Death isn't something exercised, like free speech or free assembly; it's something that simply happens to us whether we like it or not.

Rights, remember, are inalienable and endowed by the Creator. As mentioned previously, for a thing to be "inalienable" it must be something that cannot be taken away or given away. It is a condition of human existence. It clearly makes no sense to say that nonexistence is a condition of existence.

When we say we have a right *to* something, we make

a claim on it. A moral claim. We say, "By my very nature, this is mine." Yet death is not something we can take hold of and own. We cannot lay claim to death or possess it like something you can purchase at the store or have prescribed to you at the doctor's office. Death will one day claim us, not the other way around. No doubt it is scarier to think of death in these terms—as something wild, unpredictable, and untamable. Ironically, I think it's this fear of death that leads us to believe we can own it.

When I play the game hearts, I usually like to have the queen of spades in my hand to start the round. Even though it's a dangerous card, I'd much prefer to have it in my possession so that I can decide when and how it enters the game. I don't like the idea of it lurking around out there, invisible and hidden from me. It seems we treat death in a similar way. We'd rather possess it—have it in our hands to start with—than wait around for it to leap out and surprise us. But death is not a card in a game. It can't be possessed, and we shouldn't try. The only thing we can do with life is live it, and that's all we're meant to do until the matter is taken out of our hands.

We are given life, we take part in life, we participate in life, but we do not own it. We can't take possession of our lives like a two-year-old grabbing a toy from his friend and shouting "Mine!" Our lives are bigger than that, thank God. Your life is not some incidental occurrence, or an accidental mutation, or a meaningless effect in a long string of meaningless causes.

Ultimately, it's impossible to make this argument against euthanasia (although you could still make several others, which we'll cover next) without bringing God into the equation. If there is a God (and there certainly is), then our lives are not our own. God grants us the privilege and obligation of living, and reaffirms it each morning when we wake up, lungs still breathing and heart still beating. There may be times when we struggle to find the purpose or point in our existence, but if we know God, then we know there is always a purpose and a point, however obscured behind our various doubts, preoccupations, and anxieties. If there were not, we would no longer be on this earth. We cannot take our lives because our lives are not ours to take. This is an unavoidable and inarguable conclusion for anyone who believes in some kind of supernatural creative power.

I've always thought that this concept was brilliantly illustrated in the final scene of the film *Pulp Fiction*, although I don't imagine Tarantino intended that movie to be a pro-life allegory. In the last act, Samuel L. Jackson's character, Jules, is confronted by an armed robber who demands he hand over a briefcase containing a mysterious item meant for the former's boss. Jules refuses to surrender the package, even at gunpoint, coolly explaining that he can't give it because it doesn't belong to him.

So it is with our lives. I cannot destroy my life because it is not mine. It belongs to a power and authority beyond myself.

But what about those who don't believe in such a power? Well, if there is no God, then, I admit, suicide should be entirely your decision, and it doesn't really matter one way or another. If there is no God, nothing has any meaning beyond the meaning we subjectively infuse into it. Even in this case, however, it would be silly to speak of a "right to die." The doctrine of human rights springs from a belief in a God who endows us with the rights. The framework of our country is built around the idea that we have *natural* rights—rights inherent and essential to us. Rights are supernatural by definition, or at the very least metaphysical. The point is, our rights are not a physical condition, nor can they be located somewhere within our physical bodies. We talk about our rights because we believe that there is more to us than our physical bodies, and that there is more to life than this physical world.

If that is not the case, then we should stop with this "rights" foolishness. You are nothing but skin and bones and blood, and there is no transcendent quality to you that makes you entitled to free speech, or privacy, or human dignity, or anything else. In this scenario, you would certainly be welcome to kill yourself—that might really be the most logical option, to be honest—but you can't tell me you have a "right" to it. You have a right to nothing. You are a random beast, no more significant or valuable than the dirt from which you sprung.

But, I should note, even if there were no God and no reality transcending the physical world, our lives would still not belong entirely to ourselves. Whatever your spiritual beliefs, we must all see that we belong not only to ourselves but to our families and our friends and whoever else may depend upon us for care, attention, fraternity, and love.

I am not just "me"; I am also a father, husband, brother, son, and a dozen other labels that are determined by my relationship to and interactions with other people. These people do not own me like a slave, but I do, to some extent, owe myself to them. To my wife and my children, my duties are great; to my friends they are not as great; but to all I have some responsibility. My life is in many ways defined by what I am to these people. So if I were to kill myself, I would not just be killing myself. I would be murdering my daughter's father and my wife's husband and my mother's son. I wouldn't be killing one person. I'd be killing a hundred people.

2. There is nothing dignified about suicide.

The Left tells us that euthanasia enables the sick person to "die with dignity." Think of the horrible implications of that statement. If it is honorable to take an early exit, what does that say about the people who choose to live with their illnesses and afflictions until death comes on its own? If the euthanasia patient "dies with dignity," how did the cancer patient die? With shame? With dishonor?

Of course the truth is much closer to the reverse. Suicide is not dignified. One might understand the temptation in some cases, but that does not make it "dignified" for a human being to be put down like an old dog. Killing yourself to escape suffering is not brave. It is, in fact, the antithesis of bravery. If suicide is heroic, then everything we've previously called heroic isn't. In any other situation, we would say that heroism and dignity are won by marching forward despite the risk of personal pain and suffering. Nowhere else will we say that the most heroic and dignified thing is to avoid the pain at any cost.

It's said that euthanasia is dignified because it allows you to "leave on your own terms," but what does that mean? Do we somehow achieve a victory over death by using it to escape the pain of life? "Your own terms"? The terms of the drug maker who concocted the poison pill, perhaps, but your own? Hardly. None of us get to die on our own terms, because if we did then I'm sure our terms would be a perfect, happy, and healthy life, where pain and death never enter into the picture at all.

But this is not anyone's fate, because *nobody* writes the terms of their own existence. We have free will but we do

not own ourselves, and we certainly cannot take ownership of ourselves by obliterating ourselves. That would
be like trying to write a book with an eraser.

I sympathize with the desire to avoid pain, but we
should not act upon that desire. Life is to be lived like a
cup we drink until the last drop. I don't want to descend
into clichés here, but I know I'm not the only person who's
watched many a video and read many an account by and
about cancer patients who endured and fought through
the pain, and found something valuable amid it all. They
discovered that every minute meant something—in fact,
the minutes they lived in pain meant more than any of
the other minutes they'd lived in health and prosperity.

It is brave and dignified to fight, to live, to keep going
down our road until there is no more road left. That is
what we should be celebrating.

3. Euthanasia destroys the medical profession.

Since ancient times, doctors have taken the Hippocratic
oath, which outlines the core values that anyone in the
medical field should abide by. The first and most basic:
cure, heal, and treat the sick and suffering. This is the
whole point of medicine. When we accept assisted suicide, we chip away at the very foundation of the medical
field.

The obvious retort is that euthanasia can, in some

cases, count as "treating" the sick. But this is to expand the definition of "treatment" to include things that are the opposite of it.

When a patient is treated, she is offered relief and healing. *She*—the individual person—is relieved or healed. She cannot be relieved or healed if she is ended. The treatment of a person necessitates that, among other things, the person remains in existence. Euthanasia is, therefore, death *instead of* treatment, not death *as* treatment.

And as euthanasia laws eat away at the foundational principles of medicine, doctors begin to encounter a deeply problematic conflict of interest. How can they simultaneously work to fight these diseases while also helping their patients die *rather* than fight the diseases?

Time, energy, and financial resources are increasingly diverted from battling terminal illnesses to putting the terminally ill out of their misery. It's difficult to see how both avenues can be given the same attention by the same medical establishment, as they stand at odds with one another. Doctors already play both healer and executioner for babies at the earliest stages of life. Now, with the proliferation of doctor-assisted suicide, they'll be taking on those conflicting roles for the most vulnerable people at the other end of the spectrum. In these ways, the medical profession is being fundamentally redefined.

4. This is a slippery slope.

Not every slippery-slope argument is a fallacy. Sometimes it's just a matter of observing the direct consequences of a course of action. In this case, we don't even need to extrapolate or conjure up wild prophecies of what might happen if our country decides to embrace euthanasia any more than it already has.

All you need to do is look overseas, where human beings, including children, can be euthanized involuntarily. Indeed, not long ago, a mother in the UK won the right to kill her disabled daughter. The child was not terminally ill but her life, by her mother's estimation, was no longer worth living. Therefore, the girl was sentenced to death by starvation. It would be illegal to kill your livestock in such a manner, but in few countries are children protected as robustly as farm animals.

This is a logical and reasonable extension of the euthanasia argument. A doctor can only assist in a patient's suicide if certain criteria are met. Those criteria may differ by state or country, yet they all boil down to one thing: it must be agreed that the patient's life is not worth living.

Once we've made this calculation, and codified it into law, and described what sort of conditions make someone a candidate for voluntary execution, it isn't much of a leap to start applying the "solution" to people who haven't specifically consented to it.

As much as we pretend that euthanasia gives power to the patient, it really grants all of the power to the state and the medical establishment. It imbues them with the authority to decree which sort of lives are meaningful and which are not. Medical practitioners must fundamentally respect the dignity of life—not the dignity of suicide, but of life—or else they will be at odds with their own profession. If a perfectly healthy person walked into his doctor's office and asked to be put down, no doctor in any state would consent to it. The euthanasia customer must fall under certain guidelines laid out by the medical field. In other words, the doctor must agree that her life is worthless. Are we really too dense to see what sort of nightmarish conflict of interest we are encouraging here?

Imagine having stage IV cancer and visiting a doctor who, just a moment earlier, prescribed a poison pill to another person in your exact same situation. Only a moment before, this doctor said to someone, "Yes, I agree that your life should end." And now you expect him to do everything in his power to help you extend the very thing he just diagnosed as pointless?

How can we allow doctors to prescribe death? How can death ever be seen as a legitimate treatment option? If we legalize euthanasia across the country, we fundamentally change the very point and purpose of medicine. Medicine goes from something aimed at helping us live to something aimed at helping us die.

Where do you think this leads? If euthanasia is legal, and if it is only legal under certain strict circumstances, then we are saying that life, under those circumstances, is objectively undesirable. And if we say that life, under those circumstances, is objectively undesirable, then it is undesirable regardless of whether the patient desires it. The bridge from voluntary euthanasia to involuntary euthanasia is obvious. I suspect when the time comes that patients are put down whether they wish to be or not, many in our society will hardly object. We already cheer on suicide because we apparently think it foolish or even cowardly to live when suffering is inevitable and death is near. The next step is not that far a leap.

After all, suffering and death are the shared fate of all mankind. That's not the kind of cheerful sentiment I would necessarily put on a greeting card, but it is the truth nonetheless. If we believe that death is preferable to a life of unfathomable suffering, perhaps we should all be making appointments with our local death doctors.

5. Human life is valuable.

Yes, even through suffering, through sickness, through pain, through disease and disability. You might even say *especially* through sickness, pain, disease, and disability. It is a grave injustice to rob a person of whatever time they have left on this planet, and it doesn't matter how much time that happens to be.

We must all believe that, because if we didn't believe it then we'd start handing out lesser sentences to those who murder the elderly, the disabled, or the terminally ill. Indeed, if we're to look at this from a practical perspective, the thug who kills an eighty-nine-year-old woman probably only sped up the dying process by a few months or a few years. Why should he be judged as harshly as someone who kills, say, *me*?

Maybe because we don't judge the worthiness or value of a human being based on how long she's been around, or how much pain he's in, or how sad and sick she feels. At least we shouldn't judge it that way. The moment we begin to make those calculations, we forfeit any semblance of justice, compassion, and humanity.

Now, as I said, if we are nothing and we came from nothing and will return to nothing, then I suppose suicide makes some sort of sense. It returns the body to our natural state of nothingness. It brings us home into the abyss, where there is no self, no reason, no existence. But most people don't think that. Most of us are not radical nihilists. Most of us know, deep down, that there is another dimension to this reality of ours, a deeper significance beneath the surface of everything. We know that we are threads woven into the tapestry of creation—we play a role that we don't fully understand, our decisions have ramifications that we can't comprehend, and our lives have a meaning beyond whatever we find in it.

So if God reached out from the depths of eternity to hand us this life of ours, how can we think it acceptable—or worse, commendable—to throw it away before our time is finished?

Inevitably, that's what this conversation comes down to. The old questions. The oldest questions. *What is life? Why are we here? What's the point of it all?*

If you celebrate suicide, then you have answered these questions: Life is nothingness. We are here for no reason. There is no point.

If you answer differently, then you must conclude that life has *inherent value*. That's what this all comes back to. Liberals scratch their heads and wonder why some of us kooky Christians get so upset about things like abortion, euthanasia, and embryonic stem cell research. For some reason they won't listen when we try to tell them: *life has value*. It is worth something. It is worth something beyond our feelings about it, beyond circumstance, beyond context, beyond sickness, beyond development, beyond age. Life has value.

This isn't just a Christian concept. It is the concept on which Western civilization rests. Every noble ideal— justice, fairness, equity, compassion, charity—all of it, *all of it*, is grounded in the notion that human life has intrinsic value. Not value according to its usefulness, or value according to convenience, or value according to how enjoyable it is. Value. Life is valuable because it is life. If you deny this, then you deny everything. There is no reason for justice, fairness, equity, compassion, or charity if human life has no value, or merely a value contingent upon whatever parameters we've arbitrarily assigned. There can be no justification for any human right if we are simply commodities whose stock falls or rises.

This is why the war against liberalism must begin with the sanctity of life. If liberalism can redefine life—strip it of its value and its purpose—the game is over. There's nothing left to argue about. But if we engage on this battlefield, if we successfully defend the proposition that all life has meaning and dignity, then we have set the stage for victory.

5

The Abandonment of Marriage

HOW MARRIAGE GOT JILTED BY CHRISTIANS LONG BEFORE GAY RIGHTS ACTIVISTS SHOWED UP

As you're likely aware, gay marriage is, according to the federal government, a human right enshrined in the Constitution. If you're like the average American, you probably think that the Supreme Court, after about 226 years, finally found this right in the Marriage Clause of the Other Stuff You Have a Right To Amendment, which is maybe the twenty-eighth or thirtieth or somewhere around there. If you're slightly more informed than the average American, you know that the Supreme Court actually located gay marriage in the Fourteenth Amendment, which says nothing at all about gays or marriage.

But no matter how it came to be or where they found

it, here it is and here we are. A thing called gay marriage exists and, if you take society's temperature on the subject, it's apparent that this new form of "marriage" is quite lauded and celebrated in the mainstream.

The acceptance of gay marriage gives us another indication of our culture's slide back into paganism. It's often said, by both sides of the debate, that gay marriage would have seemed utterly fantastic and absurd to everyone on the planet up until very recently. That isn't exactly true. Sorry to disappoint the gay lobby, but it hasn't invented a new evil here.

Homosexuality was rife in pagan cultures, especially in ancient Greece and Rome. "Marriage" between men wasn't unheard of, either, particularly among the higher classes. The Roman emperor Nero, a murderous maniac and the first emperor to carry out the widespread persecution of Christians, "married" several members of his own sex. He would hold lavish ceremonies where he sometimes played the part of the bride. But this historical reality is not exactly helpful to the gay rights cause. Liberals using this kind of precedent to prove the legitimacy of gay marriage is like using homosexual behavior in the animal kingdom to prove the legitimacy of gay sex. Do we really want to make goats and dogs the arbiters of sexual morality? And do we really want to use the decaying pagan culture of ancient Rome as a model for ours?

The interesting thing is that the Romans lumped pederasty and homosexuality together. Homosexuality was perfectly acceptable, yes, but much of it would have been between men and their slave boys. Indeed, one of Nero's "brides" was a young boy. A look at history shows only that homosexual acceptance coincides with the rise of decadence and moral chaos. I don't think that's the point liberals really want to make, which is why they often do not protest when conservatives erroneously claim that gay marriage is unprecedented. It's not. A look at Rome is a look at our present—and our future.

A RAPID EVOLUTION

While gay marriage is not unprecedented, it has been completely rejected by Christian civilization. As the West flees Christianity and plummets back into paganism, gay marriage finds renewed favor.

This descent has been incredibly rapid. Only a few years ago, the vast majority of Americans opposed it. Gay marriage was seen in such an unfavorable light as recently as 2008 that the most liberal presidential candidate in history had to run as an advocate of "traditional marriage." He came out of the pro–gay marriage closet not long after being elected, but the fact remains that a Democrat, only a few short years ago, could not get elected to the presidency unless he affirmed man-woman marriage. Now even the most conservative Democrat would be drawn and quartered in the town square if he so much as said the phrase "traditional marriage" without the appropriate level of sneering condescension in his voice.

Many of those who identify as conservative have also reversed themselves on the issue. A 2015 Pew survey found that the number of self-described conservatives who support gay marriage had almost doubled since 2001.

Among members of my generation, Millennials, there is a virtual consensus. Those of us under the age of thirty-five who still stand for so-called traditional marriage are practically mythical creatures at this point.

The same Pew poll revealed that many mainline Protestants and Catholics have abandoned biblical notions of marriage. And for those religious groups who don't yet have a majority in favor of gay marriage, most are trending in that direction. Again, not long ago you would have been hard-pressed to find a church or religion in America whose adherents predominantly favored gay marriage. Now it's perfectly common. Seen from a historical perspective, these are shifts that happened practically overnight. Western civilization accepting gay marriage so quickly is akin to you being convinced that the moon is made of cheese after listening to someone argue the case for fourteen seconds. You now believe something that, less than half a minute ago, you would have thought mad.

Note: I use this analogy to illustrate how dramatic and sudden this transformation has been, but I realize that, in fact, a person these days probably could be convinced that the moon is made of cheese in under a minute if he saw it in a YouTube video with eerie music, and it was somehow tied in to an Illuminati conspiracy.

DIVORCED FROM OUR PRINCIPLES

Before we get into explaining why gay marriage is not real, why the definition of marriage should be protected, and why marriage serves as the foundation for the family (a lot to cover), we should first examine why we have to examine any of this to begin with. If I could travel back in time and publish this book two centuries ago, the reader would be flabbergasted that I spent page upon page explaining why marriage is between a man and a woman. In their minds, I might as well explain that fire is hot and ice is cold and marshmallows are tasty (if they had marshmallows back then, which is a subject I have not yet studied). They would consider the whole discussion a symptom of my psychosis. So why, today, has that dynamic been entirely reversed?

The broader picture is the one this book is written to address. The corrosive effects of relativism, hedonism, and secularism, advanced by the American Left through the media, Hollywood, the education system, and government, have weakened the moral fiber of our civilization and left us susceptible to attacks on our most fundamental institutions. As I've argued in previous chapters, once they were able to knock down the first pillar and redefine human life, all the rest was, absent a miraculous conservative Christian resurgence, doomed to fall with it.

Which brings us to a less comfortable reality: the lack of resistance from conservatives and Christians may have been most immediately responsible for our current situation as it pertains to marriage. That lack of resistance, the eagerness with which many Christians ceded marriage to the homosexual lobby, has its roots in many deadly trends that infiltrated the Church in the West long ago.

Let's start with divorce.

It should indeed be noted that before gay marriage was decreed by the Supreme Court, the institution of marriage had for decades already been, from a legal perspective, the least meaningful, least stable, and least protected contract in existence.

Many Christian churches gave up on the sacrament long ago, allowing their flock to divorce and remarry and divorce and remarry and divorce and remarry, and each time permitting the charade of "vows" to take place on their altars. Churches can lower the divorce rate simply by taking a consistent position on it—which is why practicing Catholics are significantly less likely to break up—but many refuse because they are cowards begging for the world's approval.

Before gay marriage, over 40 percent of America's children were already growing up without a father in the home. Statistics show that close to half of all children will witness the breakdown of their parents' marriage. Half of those half will also have the pleasure of watching a second marriage fall apart.

Most disturbing—and this, again, was happening before gay marriage—more and more young people are opting out of marriage because the previous generation was so bad at it that they've scared their kids away from the institution entirely.

Rampant divorce and remarriage eroded the institution decades before *Obergefell*. Gay marriage is perverse because, among other reasons, it removes from marriage its procreative characteristic, but the divorce epidemic takes away its permanence. Marriage is a multidimensional thing, and once you let one dimension collapse, the others are all the more vulnerable.

I should mention that there are, obviously, times when a couple has no choice but to go their separate ways. Not every divorce is an attack on the sanctity of marriage. What else can you do in cases of serial abuse or serial adultery, or when one party simply abandons the other? But infidelity and abuse do not explain the majority of divorces in this country, and they are not the leading causes of breakups.

A survey done by the National Fatherhood Initiative found finances and lack of communication to be the leading culprits. An article in the *Washington Examiner* also cites finances as the most potent divorce fuel. According to any survey on the subject, other top causes of divorce are a lack of individual identity, getting into it for the wrong reasons, and becoming lost in the roles.

In other words, these days, marriages can be blown apart by the slightest gust of wind, coming from any direction, and for any reason. It's no wonder gay marriage became such a hit so fast. Divorce and gay marriage are not the same thing, and the former is not as direct an attack on the sanctity of marriage because it can be necessary in some circumstances, whereas the latter is not necessary, and, as I'll explain, not even possible under any circumstance. But once we accept that a person can enter into a succession of permanent and indissoluble bonds with different partners, and that each successive "permanent" bond can be forged while the previous partner is still alive, despite the "until death do us part" maxim we spoke so confidently in our vows, we certainly have compromised our ability to credibly stand for "one man, one woman" marriage.

A BITTER PILL

While gay marriage, as I mentioned, removes the procreative characteristic from marriage, we must address the giant, barren elephant in the room and acknowledge that many married heterosexual couples choose to remove that characteristic on their own. Along with divorce, contraception gained mainstream acceptance in the Christian community decades ago, and paved the way for gay activists to eventually make their move.

The first birth control pill was approved by the FDA in 1960, and no drug—not heroin, not crack cocaine, not anything—has had a more devastating impact on our society. You could write a book—and plenty of people have—on how the pill helped precipitate our cultural decline, but for the purposes of this discussion we should concentrate on its deteriorating effects on marriage.

There's been a lot of research done on how hormonal birth control has changed women's taste in men. A paper published in the journal *Trends in Ecology and Evolution* detailed how women on the pill tend to gravitate toward men who are more feminine. This explains, in part, the pop-culture devolution from Frank Sinatra to Justin Bieber, Clint Eastwood to Zac Efron, and so forth. The pill, being a chemical substance that so profoundly messes with a woman's biology, creates confusion and pulls her toward men she wouldn't otherwise find attractive. This has been a great boon for effeminate men who wear skinny jeans and drink low-fat lattes, but the rest have found the dating scene much more difficult because of it.

A study in the *Proceedings of the National Academy of Sciences* found that a woman's physical attraction to her husband may suddenly diminish or disappear if she meets him while on the pill and then goes off it at some point during their marriage. From the *Time* article about the study:

> Whether a woman's attraction to her mate shifted post-Pill seemed to be determined by how objectively good-looking he was by evolutionary standards, which means his attractiveness is an indicator of genetic fitness. Some women with partners who were not conventionally attractive reported being less attracted to him after stopping oral contraceptives, whereas a decrease was not seen in women whose partners were conventionally handsome.

On the flip side, a woman on the pill may not be as attracted to her strikingly handsome and masculine husband as she would be if she stopped taking the pill. (Luckily, my wife is not on birth control, so she is able to admire my beauty unimpeded by chemical interference.)

Additionally, a 2008 article in *Scientific American* reported on the results of multiple studies finding that women on birth control prefer men who are genetically similar to them:

> Hidden in a man's smell are clues about his major histocompatibility complex (MHC) genes, which play an important role in immune system surveillance. Studies suggest that females prefer the scent of males whose MHC genes differ from their own, a preference that has probably evolved because it helps offspring survive . . .
>
> A study published in August in the *Proceedings of the Royal Society B*, however, suggests that women on the pill undergo a shift in preference toward men who share similar MHC genes.

It's no surprise that birth control has such a profound and confounding impact on a woman's psyche. The primary function of the pill is to essentially trick her body into believing she's pregnant all the time. It doesn't take a scientist to surmise that perhaps a woman's body is not meant to be, or to believe itself to be, perpetually pregnant for thirty years. And, as a married man with three children, I can attest that pregnancy can be, at times—and I say this cautiously—a rather emotionally tumultuous time for a lady. And that's just over the course of a nine-month pregnancy. I tremble with fear at the thought of what effect a 360-month pregnancy could have on my wonderful wife.

This is one, though not the only, reason why the rates of birth control usage and divorce track almost identically. As the pill gained prevalence, so did divorce. That doesn't necessarily prove anything, and you certainly can't blame a pill for your decision to get divorced, but it's a correlation that no honest person can ignore. It's hard to see it as a complete coincidence that the sexual revolution and the divorce epidemic took hold in the 1960s, the decade that began with FDA approval of the pill.

It's true that, although birth control usage is near ubiquitous today, the divorce rate has actually been declining for some time. According to an article in the *New York Times* in 2014, if current trends continue, about two-thirds of marriages that began in the 2000s will not end in divorce. Of course, that means a third of marriages will dissolve—hardly a reason to pop the champagne and pat ourselves on the back—but at least a third is less than the erroneous "half of all marriages will end in divorce" statistic that many people still cite.

But this can hardly be seen as a vindication of the pill or an indication that the marriage crisis in America is over. Perhaps there are fewer (but still a great many) people getting divorced, yet at the same time there are far fewer adults choosing marriage to begin with. Today, there are twice as many unmarried adults as there were in 1960. A recent Pew report estimated that a quarter of Millennials will never get married at all. It seems we've figured out a way to avoid divorce: avoid marriage. It's like we're bragging that we figured out how to avoid spraining our ankles by simply staying in bed and watching Netflix all day. Hardly an inspiring victory.

Despite our culture's shortcut around the divorce problem, there are ways to shield your marriage from divorce while still actually getting married in the first place. One tip may be to dump the pill. Among couples who use natural family planning instead of artificial birth control, the divorce rate is, astoundingly, less than 3 percent.

Why the stark contrast between the two methods? I'd surmise that it has something to do with the fact that natural family planning requires trust, discipline, and self-control, and marriage requires all of that, too. It turns out that we should bring into our sex lives all of the things that should be brought into our marriage as a whole. And the more we do that, it seems, the more we protect ourselves from divorce. Treating sex like something purely recreational ultimately weakens its significance, which weakens our marriage, which weakens us, which is all very fortunate for divorce attorneys.

Contraception is a mutual barrier placed between the spouses. It is a shared rejection not only of children, but of each other. It says, "I will give only so much." But marriages cannot survive if we will give only so much. The whole point of the union, and of the sexual act that strengthens and deepens that union, is to give everything to the other, holding nothing back, and embracing whatever fruits may grow from our love for and devotion to each other. The spirit of marriage is diminished when we refuse to enthusiastically accept all that naturally comes with it. Aside from the emotional, psychological, and physical toll birth control can have on a woman, it's the spiritual effect that is really the most devastating.

The pill also commodifies and degrades women by tying their human worth to their economic worth. Proponents of the pill essentially say that women must sterilize themselves, whether permanently or temporarily, in order to "succeed" in the business world. Her value as a woman, as a human being, is placed below her value as an employee or a consumer. Male employees may often feel the same way, but they are not expected to chemically alter themselves or to reject their own fertility in order to be a cog in the corporate system. Only women are burdened with that expectation. I am rarely one to play the "S card," but perhaps this is where we ought to be looking in search of workplace sexism.

I can tell you this: if scientists ever develop a birth control pill for men that renders them impotent, potentially causes cancer, requires them to take a dose every day, and makes their testicles shrivel, I can guarantee that that drug would not be among Rite Aid's best sellers. Even the men who love the female birth control pill would suddenly find the whole idea rather distasteful and degrading.

But the most relevant thing about the birth control pill is that it, of course, stops procreation.

Many people—Christians included—now believe that a woman is "liberated" when she treats her reproductive system like a disease that can only be cured by pumping her body full of chemicals that inhibit ovulation. Which is to say, she is liberated by causing her body to malfunction and preventing it from doing what it is naturally meant to do.

(Odd that these days, we won't even eat an avocado if we find out any aspect of its harvesting and cultivation involved something inorganic, yet we rarely apply those convictions to the highly potent mix of synthetic hormones many women consume on a near-daily basis for years and years of their lives.)

At any rate, as Christians we know that our bodies are temples of the Holy Spirit (1 Corinthians 6:19), and we know that God's first commandment to man was "Be fruitful and multiply" (Genesis 1:28). But many of us became just as hooked on the drug as anyone else, so there was hardly anyone left to make these points.

Christians, in the main, decided that marriage did not have to be *necessarily* procreative, and at the same time they decided it did not have to be *necessarily* permanent, and when the gay activists came along, what argument did they have left? Granted, just because a person is a hypocrite doesn't make him wrong about what he's saying—a man could have five divorces under his belt and he'd still be right if he described marriage as a sacred, imperishable bond—but it's harder to argue convincingly for a principle when you don't believe it. And it's even harder to defend an institution while personally rejecting most parts of it yourself.

This is a reality Christians often have trouble facing. Our culture did not slip away from us in the middle of the night. Our institutions weren't ripped down suddenly by the barbarian hordes. Although I am writing about the Left's assault on life, marriage, and gender, it should be made very clear that we are not victims of the assault. We are participants. Marriage is probably the best example of this. Christians were so inconsistent on the subject—our arguments purposefully incomplete so as to allow loopholes to accommodate our own extrabiblical lifestyle choices—that we'd already ensured there would be little to no chance the marriage ideal in America could survive a sustained attack from the Left.

6

The Impossibility of Same-Sex Marriage

WHY "GAY MARRIAGE" IS
A CONTRADICTION IN TERMS

Now that we know how we ended up with gay marriage, we can awkwardly transition into a conversation about why there is no gay marriage. There is no such thing as gay marriage and there can never be any such thing as gay marriage. "Gay" is simply not a modifier that can be attached to "marriage."

We have something we call gay marriage, but the entire problem with gay marriage existing is that it can't exist. There can no more be gay marriage than there can be a rounded square or a triangular cube. And if the government set out to decree that a circle is a square or that a triangle is a cube, I would oppose it for the same reason

I oppose gay marriage. Although squares would remain squares and cubes cubes, the effect such a law would have on the field of geometry would be similar to the effect gay marriage has on the institution of marriage.

It's important to establish that the argument is about the nature of marriage, not the nature of law or human rights or love or anything else. It is a bit late now, years after gay marriage was enacted across the land by Supreme proclamation, to finally clarify what the argument was actually about, but if we ever hope to legally restore the "traditional" definition of marriage, we must be clear on this point. The defenders of the "traditional" definition, as we've seen, largely gave up defending it, and many of those who remained were not effective because they did not understand what they were defending.

So, two notes of clarification at the outset.

1. Nobody ever wanted to make gay marriage illegal.

You'll notice that nobody—at least from what I saw— went around insisting that gay marriage be "prohibited" or "criminalized." That's because the argument over whether gay marriage should be legal or illegal is a false dichotomy, constructed and promoted by progressives and gay activists. They rather successfully framed it as an argument between two different but valid versions of marriage. You have "traditional marriage" on one side and "gay marriage" on the other. According to progressives, the traditional-marriage proponents are bullies who want to exclude the gay version of marriage.

But the object was never to make gay marriage illegal but rather to communicate that it is not possible. Marriage is, fundamentally, intrinsically, inherently, in principle, the permanent monogamous union between members of the opposite sex. That is what it is. Marriage is a thing. An Actual, Real Thing. And as An Actual, Real Thing, it has characteristics and qualities; it has a concrete purpose, an objective function.

It was always the purpose, function, and characteristic of marriage that "excluded" gays, never the law. We'll return to the true nature of marriage later on in this chapter.

All the proponents of "traditional marriage" were asking for was a government that recognizes the reality of marriage. That was certainly not a plea for more government "involvement" or government intrusion, but for less. For the State to ratify, acknowledge, and afford a special status to the marriage between a man and a woman isn't "intrusive." After all, the government recognizes me as a human being, doesn't it? I don't feel intruded upon just because the State affords me the legal status of a person, rather than, say, a houseplant or a porcupine.

I don't want the government "involved" in my marriage. I am not asking for a state-appointed representative to come to my house and oversee the whole arrangement. What I want is for the government to simply recognize the institution, generally speaking, because it is a real thing and an important thing and there is no credible reason for the government to deny its existence. There is nothing wrong with the State saying, "Our country needs children, children need parents, and parents need to be married to provide stability for their children, so we will do certain things to protect and encourage this valuable institution." The only problem is that it offends the emotional sensibilities of some people, but that is not actually a real problem. It is a problem only for the person who is offended, and her problem should not be our problem.

The real intrusion or "involvement" occurs when the government decides not to recognize things for what they are. It's when human beings aren't recognized as human beings—like unborn humans, for instance—that the government intrudes. The intrusion is when the State ignores or attempts to change or pervert the nature of something. That's when you get slavery, abortion, and yes, gay marriage.

2. I am not and never was a proponent of "traditional marriage."

In fact, it was a grave mistake that we ever started using the phrase. I've used it in this chapter already several times, which shows how effective the Left can be at framing the debate. Even when I argue against how they frame the debate, I'm still arguing according to how they framed it.

Just as there is no such thing as gay marriage, there is no such thing as traditional marriage.

You wouldn't take your kids to the zoo and say, "Oh look, kids, it's a traditional penguin," would you?

You don't go to the doctor and say, "Doc, my traditional elbow hurts," do you?

If your child is doing his math homework and writes down that 2 + 2 = 4, you don't say, "Yes, that's traditional arithmetic," do you?

No, because to tack "traditional" onto something is to imply that there are completely legitimate nontraditional versions of it.

Traditional marriage isn't traditional—it's real, it's actual, it's marriage. It's the only kind that exists or can ever exist.

Marriage isn't a flavor of barbecue sauce. Yes, there are traditional barbecue sauces and ones infused with different spices and flavors, and they're all still entirely barbecue sauces. But that's not marriage. Marriage is no more "traditional" than gravity is traditional. We shouldn't refer to "traditional marriage" any more than we should look down at the splattered remains of someone who jumped out a window and say, "I guess they have traditional gravity around here."

That's because gravity is gravity. Gravity is a reality. So is marriage. There is marriage, and there is not marriage. Two men living together is not marriage. It's not *untraditional* marriage—it's just not marriage.

I would say the same about "biblical marriage." It was a mistake—again, I know I'm Monday-morning quarterbacking this thing—to push so heavily on how the Bible defines marriage.

It is true, of course, that Christ himself defines it as a union between a man and a woman. From Matthew 19:

> *And He answered and said to them, "Have you not read that He who made them at the beginning 'made them male and female,' and said, 'For this reason a man shall leave his father and mother and be joined to his wife, and the two shall become one flesh'? So then, they are no longer two but one flesh. Therefore what God has joined together, let not man separate."*

It's also true that Scripture expressly forbids and condemns the homosexual act. 1 Corinthians 6:9–11:

> *Or do you not know that the unrighteous will not inherit the kingdom of God? Do not be deceived: neither the sexually immoral, nor idolaters, nor adulterers, nor men who practice homosexuality, nor thieves, nor the greedy, nor drunkards, nor revilers, nor swindlers will inherit the kingdom of God. And such were some of you.*

But you were washed, you were sanctified, you were justified in the name of the Lord Jesus Christ and by the Spirit of our God.

And there's Romans 1:26–28:

For this reason God gave them up to dishonorable passions. For their women exchanged natural relations for those that are contrary to nature; and the men likewise gave up natural relations with women and were consumed with passion for one another, men committing shameless acts with men and receiving in themselves the due penalty for their error. And since they did not see fit to acknowledge God, God gave them up to a debased mind to do what ought not to be done.

And 1 Timothy 1:10:

The sexually immoral, men who practice homosexuality, enslavers, liars, perjurers, and whatever else is contrary to sound doctrine . . .

And so on.

But the truth of marriage is innate and accessible to all people, even those who have not read the Bible. We are discussing the nature of a human institution, its purpose, its function—this is not just a religious matter but a scientific and social one. The Bible provides great insight into this, but the truth of marriage is not true simply because the Bible said it. On the contrary, the Bible said it because it's true.

It makes sense to talk about biblical marriage with Christians who deny what Scripture has to say on the subject. As believers we are commanded to acquiesce to the Word of God even if we do not agree, so those Christians should be reminded of their apostasy. But we were never going to convince the secular world to respect marriage by quoting Corinthians or throwing barbs from Leviticus. And the more we presented marriage as a matter of religious conviction, the more we vindicated their view that our opinion on marriage was just a product of religious conviction.

With those stipulations registered for the record, we can examine this "nature of marriage" thing I keep yammering on about.

THE NATURE OF MARRIAGE

Marriage is by definition between a man and a woman. That isn't an arbitrary designation. It isn't fueled by hate. It isn't bigotry. It isn't intolerance. The union between a man and a woman, in principle, has a power and a capacity that no other union could ever possess. For this reason it certainly is not "equal" to any other union.

A man and a woman can create other humans. They

can form families. They can bring forth life. This difference is not an aberration or a matter of mere semantics. It's something important, serious, and profound. It's a matter of biological and anatomical truth to say that men and women were literally designed for one another.

Today we see children as a "punishment," to use Barack Obama's infamous phrase, or as a potential obstacle to be hurdled on the path toward sexual gratification. But the fact that a human life can be brought into existence through this relationship is, if nothing else, a sign that men and women are made to be compatible with one another. And it's a sign that this compatibility is tremendously important, as the propagation of humanity depends on it. No other relationship bears that responsibility, and so no other relationship needs to be, or should be, put on an equal pedestal with it.

The man-woman relationship has a potential and a capacity that is completely unique. It has attributes that cannot be emulated by any other form of human relationship. In light of this, most societies have afforded it a certain respect, out of both necessity and sound philosophy, and this bond was given a name: *marriage*.

Marriage is the context in which families are formed and maintained. That's why it's important. That's why it's different. To "open up" the definition of marriage to include relationships—even relationships between individuals who share a strong emotional connection—that do not share these essential components is to actively undermine the family.

Marriage is the union between man and woman—two different but complementary people—made one flesh by the rite of matrimony, and bound together by their vows and their shared responsibility to create and maintain a properly ordered family. That is how marriage was defined in Western civilization for millennia. Gay marriage does not expand this definition. It abolishes it.

OUT WITH THE OLD, IN WITH NOTHING

You'll notice, by the way, that proponents of the new definition haven't—except for tax purposes—actually offered a new definition. They've made their opposition to the "traditional" one known, but they will not suggest an alternative. For all this talk about the definition of marriage, it's rather striking that only one side ever offered one.

If there is no alternative definition, if liberals cannot define this new thing they've created, then they must publicly admit their intention to obliterate the institution, not simply to "redefine" it. If they wish to keep the institution, however, then they must explain where the new lines will be drawn and—importantly—why.

Definitions require lines of distinction. If I'm going to define the word *up*, for instance, then I must come up with a definition that rudely excludes down. If I want to define *cow*, I must have a definition that discriminates against horses and aardvarks.

The "old" version of marriage drew a clear, obvious, logical, purposeful, meaningful, and objective line. What about the new? Is marriage merely a romantic agreement between two individuals who love each other? If so, that opens up a whole slew of alternate manifestations of marriage, which either leaves the definition so "open" as to fade it into oblivion, or else it requires the pioneers of this edited thing to begin making a thousand stipulations until, before long, they're doing exactly what they accused us of doing, only they're now doing it for increasingly arbitrary and superficial reasons.

IF GAY MARRIAGE, THEN PEDOPHILIA

They don't like it when we say this, but it's true: if marriage is not between one man and one woman, then you have to tell us what it is instead, and whatever it is, you won't be able to include gay marriage in the new definition without letting things like incest and pedophilia and bestiality through the gate.

Yes, that's an argument you've heard before. It's a slippery-slope cliché. It's offensive and insensitive. It's also valid and unassailable. Really, this argument is an argument about arguments. It argues that the arguments you use in one scenario must be applied equally to all other relevant scenarios.

It works like this:

If you assert that X justifies A, then you have not only argued for A as an end but also for X as a means. You have said, "A is true and right, and I know that A is true and right because X is a legitimate way to ascertain the truth and rightness of something."

I may then test both your end and your means by experimenting with X to see if it could also apply to a thing—Z—that we both find abhorrent. If it does, then either you were wrong about A or you were wrong that X justifies A—or you must accept that, in arguing for A, you have also argued for Z.

I feel like this is becoming an algebra equation, and as someone who needs a calculator to divide six by three, I fear I'm out of my league. Why don't we examine this principle in a real-world situation?

Let's say a Muslim challenges me to explain why it's morally acceptable to consume pork. Let's say I'm a horrible debater, so I defend my pig-eating ways by saying simply, "It tastes good and I like it." If that's the only argument I have at my intellectual disposal, the Muslim could easily win the argument and defeat my reasoning by pointing out that a cannibal probably eats a human because it tastes good and he likes it.

This astute challenger will have backed me into a

rhetorical corner. Or, more accurately, I've backed myself into a corner by claiming that an act can be morally justified based on how much I enjoy it. This would force me to either come up with a better line of reasoning (I could say that I really hated the movie *Babe* and I think all pigs should die as retribution), or I'd have to accept his premise that I'm basically Jeffrey Dahmer because I had a pulled pork sandwich last Tuesday. What I can't do is simply roll my eyes and say, "Yeah, but that's, like, totally different."

A vague dismissal does not a valid argument make. If you're trying to challenge an age-old concept or drastically change an ancient institution, you need arguments for doing so that include your new amendment but still preclude other amendments that even you would find abhorrent.

G. K. Chesterton put it this way: "In the matter of reforming things, as distinct from deforming them, there is one plain and simple principle; a principle which will probably be called a paradox. There exists in such a case a certain institution or law; let us say, for the sake of simplicity, a fence or gate erected across a road. The more modern type of reformer goes gaily up to it and says, 'I don't see the use of this; let us clear it away.' To which the more intelligent type of reformer will do well to answer: 'If you don't see the use of it, I certainly won't let you clear it away. Go away and think. Then, when you can come back and tell me that you do see the use of it, I may allow you to destroy it.'"

The point is clear here. Gay marriage proponents want to tear down the fence, even though they don't understand why it's there. But when they tear it down, they're going to want to rebuild it somewhere a bit farther down the road. But because they don't know why it was put there in the first place, they won't know where to put it now.

What we know for certain is that a thing cannot have two fundamental natures. A circle cannot be a square; even less can it be a circle and a square at the same time. A thing cannot be two things at once, and it cannot be denied that gay marriage and true marriage are two different things. Even those who do not see a moral or social problem with homosexual unions cannot honestly suggest that they notice nothing distinctive about heterosexual marriage.

AN OBVIOUS DISTINCTION

To be clear, the distinctions are as follows:

(1) **One involves people of the same sex; the other does not.**

(2) **In one there is never any possibility of procreation; in the other there is.**

Those are a couple of solid differences. You may call them irrelevant, but you cannot say they are not differences. You may say they are insignificant, but you cannot say they are fictitious.

But are they in fact insignificant and irrelevant?

It's fascinating that we would ask such a question. This is a country where we go out and buy new iPhones because they're slightly different from the iPhones we bought fourteen months ago. We pay for upgraded seats on an airplane because they're slightly better than the seats three rows back. We cry discrimination and persecution if we find out that our coworker makes slightly more than us, or has a slightly bigger office or a slightly more comfortable chair. We purchase TVs for a slightly clearer picture. In other words, we find immense, world-shattering connotations in the faintest little cosmetic changes and deviations, yet we struggle to appreciate the difference between heterosexual and homosexual couples, a difference that, if I must remind you, involves the creation of human life.

A man and a woman can get together and make a person. They can, between the two of them, conceive a human child. If I have to put this in terms that my fellow nostalgic Millennials will comprehend: a man and a woman can combine their powers, much like the Power Rangers, and create a brand-new thing. Maybe a better analogy would be *Captain Planet*, where all the Planeteers could combine forces and conjure a separate sentient being (though the being conjured by marriage usually isn't a spandex-clad vigilante who goes around assaulting people for throwing aluminum cans into the wrong wastebasket).

The two relationships differ from each other. They are not equal. One is something, the other is something else. They are not the same.

PROCREATIVE IN PRINCIPLE

Yes, to answer the standard objection, it's true that not all married heterosexual couples can have kids. It's also true that, as we covered in the last chapter, quite a number of them choose not to have kids. But does that render moot the principle that marriage is by definition procreative?

Well, let's look at it this way: Is it accurate to say, in principle, that human beings have legs?

If so, what about a person born legless or a person who loses her legs in a tragic accident later in life?

Is she now subhuman?

Does she belong to some other species?

What about lazy couch potatoes who choose not to use their legs, electing instead to sit on the couch and watch *Top Chef* reruns?

Do any of these examples falsify my "human beings have legs" statement?

Or do they simply reflect the fact that humans have

free will and that the human body is prone to disease and dysfunction?

Some heterosexual couples can't conceive children. This happens by disability, mutation, defect, or some other physical misfortune, but we most often call it a defect precisely because we recognize that there is a procreative potential these individuals should share but do not, through no fault of their own.

These people can't have kids incidentally, whereas two men or two women can't have kids by the very nature of their union. One is an accident of nature—an aberration—while the other is a result of nature.

THERE IS ONLY ONE TYPE OF FAMILY

What about gay couples adopting children? Surely adoption means that gay couples can still fulfill the purpose and nature of marriage.

Well, even if it were true that gay adoption is healthy for children, it would not make gay marriage legitimate. You can't any more make a walrus into a human by stitching human legs onto his hide than you can make a human nonhuman by removing his legs.

Regardless, the most exhaustive studies have categorically proven that same-sex parenting is not equal to heterosexual parenting, and that children of gay couples are more likely to grow up with emotional difficulties.

This is not surprising. The psychological benefits of having a dad and a mom in the home are clear and incontrovertible. Forty years of research into the subject demonstrates the inescapable and self-evident reality that children *need* fathers and mothers.

The book *Marriage on Trial* by Glenn T. Stanton and Dr. Bill Maier reports that babies can tell the difference between a male and a female by eight weeks of age:

> This diversity in itself provides children with a broader, richer experience of contrasting relational interactions. . . . Whether they realize it or not, by sheer experience children are learning at the earliest age that men and women are different and have different ways of dealing with most aspects of life.

It's obvious that mothers and fathers bring something different and diverse to the table. This is not just an assumption but an indisputable scientific fact, backed by years of research and millennia of human experience. Indeed, over 350 studies from over a dozen nations confirm the importance of a household with both parents present.

When looking at any indicator, from general happiness to professional success to educational achievement, the essential need for a child to have the input of a mother and a father is demonstrable and unmistakable.

A child has a right to a mom and a dad. If she cannot have that because her parents are dead or otherwise out of the picture, and she is waiting to be adopted, then the next best option is for her to be taken in by a new family where the father role can be filled by a man and the mother role by a woman. What is natural and intended should be re-created, not subverted or replaced by something disordered and disorienting.

Of course, some children don't have both parents because they live in single-parent homes. Whether by death or divorce or abandonment, they are left with just their mother or their father. These children are not doomed, obviously, and their lives can still be extremely happy and fulfilling, but nobody would call this an ideal scenario.

The point is, no matter what, all kids—everyone, all people, everywhere, forever—have an innate longing to be connected with and raised by both a male and female parental figure. Preferably, these figures would be their biological progenitors. But if this cannot be the case, then ideally they'd have another male and female to fill that void.

The confusion sets in when a child does not have, say, his father around, and then another female separate from his mother comes in to take up that position. The kid will still long for that male influence, and the more that it isn't fulfilled by his mom's female lover, the more bewildered and disturbed and guilty he will likely feel. At least if he had a single mom, nobody would tell him that he *shouldn't* desire a male role model. But the children of gay couples are told every day, whether explicitly or implicitly, that they should be perfectly happy with two moms or two dads.

Gay couples, on the other hand, do not have a right to be parents, because kids are not property or fashion statements. Kids have rights. And among them is the right to not be tossed into the middle of a social experiment that tinkers with the most fundamental characteristics of the family. They have a right to a stable home life. It may be true that heterosexual unions often end in divorce these days, but the answer is to strengthen those unions, not abandon them. Besides, whatever the divorce rates say, the fact is that gay couples, particularly men, are very often not monogamous. Although infidelity occurs among straight couples, among gay couples it is part of the lifestyle.

Studies out of San Francisco State University and Alliant International University concluded that approximately 50 percent of male homosexual relationships are "open," meaning the partners are allowed to have other partners on the side. In half of all gay relationships, there is not, apparently, even an attempt at fidelity.

A study by the Amsterdam Municipal Health Service, published in 2003, found that the average gay relationship lasts less than two years. Other research has found that over 80 percent of gay men have had over fifty sexual partners in their lifetime, with close to 30 percent estimating that they've been with more than a thousand. A *thousand*, for God's sake.

Throw in the fact that gays have much higher rates of alcoholism, drug abuse, and disease, and you begin to see that perhaps this is a catastrophic environment in which to raise a family.

Children require constancy and stability. They need to feel that they have a solid foundation under their feet. To throw them into a world characterized by temporary flings and polyamorous love triangles is to deprive them of the safety and security they deserve and desire. Admittedly, many children raised by heterosexual couples are not given this kind of stability either, but the gay community has all of these flaws on steroids. And the one thing a gay couple can, in principle, never provide, and the one thing all children need more than anything else, is the love and attention of a devoted mother and father, each playing a role and serving a purpose the other cannot.

THE HOMOSEXUAL CHOICE

Another argument raised by progressives is that homosexuality is innate—not a choice or a decision—which proves that it is natural, which proves, allegedly, that gay marriage is itself natural. I'll briefly address this argument because it is common, not because it's compelling. Obviously, even if homosexuals were "born with it," that doesn't say anything about the nature of marriage. Just because you are born with a desire for something does not mean you should have it or can have it. I was born with a desire to fly, but that doesn't mean I can barge into the cockpit of a commercial aircraft and help myself to the captain's chair. And suppose I do; I doubt my arguments about my innate desires would hold a lot of weight during the FBI investigation.

In any case, it isn't quite true that gays are gay from birth. There are many factors that play into our sexual orientation. It isn't written entirely into our genetic code—it develops over time, and it can change. Some of it has nothing to do with our choices; some of it does. The idea of someone being gay from birth brings to mind the somewhat questionable concept of homosexual babies lusting after other babies of the same sex. It should go without saying that there can't really be any gay two-year-olds running around out there because children that age aren't sexually attracted to anyone or anything. Their sexuality will manifest itself gradually as they grow older, which is a big part of that whole puberty thing.

Of course, this process is influenced by environment and culture and hormones *and choice*. For instance, a young boy exposed to graphic pornography from a young age will likely develop sexual urges that are different from one who isn't (what precious few exist in that latter category). That doesn't mean one will be gay and one won't; it just means one will be different from the other. After all, this isn't just a gay-versus-straight thing. As the bespectacled feminist sitting in a gender studies class right now might say, orientation isn't "binary."

These days we even have folks sexually aroused by inanimate objects and furry mascots and anime. Was that written into their genes from birth? Were they fated to that "lifestyle"? Was the anime enthusiast designed by God to find sexual fulfillment in cartoons? Or were these people exposed to images and activities that helped to develop and solidify those attractions—which they then made the decision to indulge in?

I'm not dogmatic about this, personally. Everyone seems to be looking for the easy answer, but I'm not. We are all inclined certain ways; we have certain urges— I'm not just talking sexually, but generally—and these impulses can be traced back to everything from our upbringing, to our hormones, to our culture, to our biology, to the media we consume, to, yes, our choices.

The proliferation of pornography does have the effect of, in essence, spreading perversion like herpes at a jamband festival. We are so sexually overexposed and overstimulated from such a young age that we grow weary of healthy and natural sexuality years before we even become sexually active. Like drug addicts, we search for new highs. In that stale boredom, we delve into all kinds of filth and depravity, and as those seeds of perversion grow in our minds, we water them by finding "communities" of people online who share an enthusiasm for the same brand of debauchery. In my view, this is another reason why people "become gay." Because there's nothing else to do.

I was equal parts engrossed and repulsed recently when I read an interview online with a leading member and documentarian of the burgeoning "furry" community. For those who are not aware of this disturbed subset of the population, I will now, in order to illustrate my point, ruin your day by telling you about them. The furries are grown adults—mostly men and, according to the man in the interview, mostly gay—who dress up in animal costumes and attend conventions and gatherings where they connect with other costumed fetishists. They have sex, of course, and do other strange things, the details of which are best left to be conjured in the darkest recesses of the reader's imagination.

What's relevant about this troubled man's story is that it started, of course, online, where he began watching porn as a child. Somehow or another, during one of his pubescent porn binges, he happened across a video or photographs of furry beings humping. He found that this intrigued his confused and overstimulated twelve-year-old self, and after a while, as he plunged deeper into this world of furry weirdos, he realized that there was a whole "community" of people who get their rocks off to the same thing. Now, being a furry is his identity, he says. It's who he is. He considers himself even more a furry than he does a homosexual.

But are we to believe that this twisted infatuation with sexualized animal costumes was embedded into his genes from birth? Or is it possible that he developed the fetish as a child because it was different and strange and he was lost and bored, his mind hopelessly saturated in the filth of online pornography? Then, when he began to feel shame and disgust at these inclinations, he took comfort in the fact that many other people apparently indulge in the same bizarre fantasies. Thus, he was effectively "turned" into a furry, where if he'd been reading books or skipping stones down at the creek rather than masturbating to graphic pornography during his formative years, he may have grown into a perfectly normal, healthy, heterosexual adult.

Being gay is not exactly like being a furry, or being a member of whatever other fetish community, but I think the process often follows along the same lines. Certain urges are developed and sort of fertilized at a young age, and eventually a person finds not only sexual gratification in those urges, but identity.

So the big questions are: Are we defined by our urges or by our actions? Are we compelled to turn our desires into a "lifestyle," or can we live beyond them? Do our proclivities automatically become a state of being?

I would say no, and so in that sense, it *is* a choice whether to be gay or to be straight. Our feelings may not be up to us, but how we live, what we do, whether we indulge those feelings—these decisions are ours to make.

Take the example of men who experience same-sex attraction but choose to resist it, control it, and even marry women and have kids. In today's culture we are supposed to pretend these men don't exist, or that they exist as traitors to "their people," but I don't see them that way. I see them as men who sometimes *feel* one way but choose to *be* another way.

Progressivism, on the other hand, insists that you are what you feel, and that what you feel is entirely out of your hands; you are a slave to your emotions and desires (but remember, not to your gender, because that's the one negotiable here). This is another defining characteristic of their ideology; it turns you inward and tells you to never attempt to transcend your base urges.

WHAT'S LOVE GOT TO DO WITH IT?

So we know that "gay marriage" and "traditional marriage" are fundamentally distinct concepts, and we know that the distinction is deep and important; we know that there is no way to compensate for the differences; and we know that the gays are not fated to the lifestyle from birth (and even if they were, it would be irrelevant to the question). What is left, then? How can "gay marriage" and "traditional marriage" share the same title when they share nothing else and have no other similarities?

The standard response is "love." Two men have a "right" to love each other, just the same as a man and a woman. But there are problems here: First, the love is not the same between the two respective couples. The love between a man and a woman gives birth to civilization. It creates life. It makes families. The love between a man and a woman is the bedrock. The foundation. The root that grounds our society and sustains it.

The love between men is not procreative. It does not conceive and bring forth life. It does not do anything, practically speaking. A fraternal love between men can be enriching in its own way, but a sexual relationship is, far from procreative and organic, destructive and un-natural. The sky-high rates of drug abuse, depression, disease, and suicide in the gay community ought to prove this point. Just as one example, a 2008 study published in the medical journal *BMC Psychiatry* found that the suicide rate is 200 percent higher for men who've been involved in sexual relationships with other men.

Second, as scandalous as this may seem to those

who've ingested a steady diet of Nicholas Sparks novels and 1990s romantic comedies starring Meg Ryan, marriage is not just about love. Certainly, society's rooting interest in your marriage has nothing to do with how you feel about your wife or your husband. Love is not hinged on how you feel, but on the choices you make. Love is itself a choice, as the old saying goes.

It's revealing that our culture considers the emotional sensation of love to be the essence of marriage. This is why you end up with all of those divorces we talked about, and also why you end up with so many young men and women choosing cohabitation over marriage. If you love each other—that is, if you have nice feelings toward one another—there is no reason to get married, because you are already experiencing marriage, for all intents and purposes. Likewise, if you're married and the emotions fade, you may as well move on. Marriage is supposed to feel good, and now that it doesn't, it has no purpose. Time to cut your losses. The kids will understand.

But true marital love—the kind that society has a stake in, the kind that must be given a name, that must become its own institution—is more than emotional attachment or infatuation. Those are fleeting things. Marital love is committed, indissoluble, and procreative. Even if the feelings fade for a time, the love—that choice to remain loyal, to remain one, together for the sake of the other and the children—persists. If your relationship is not ordered toward family and commitment, there truly is no reason to stay in it if it should stop making you feel good. This, again, is what separates marriage from all other relationships, and it's why only a man and a woman may enter into it.

Of course, the critic may say: OK, so the marriage between a man and a woman is different from the marriage between two men or two women, and the difference is quite essential. Fine. But should the government codify that difference by awarding the marriage title only to heterosexual couples? Why shouldn't the government just stay out of it entirely?

Because the government doesn't award marriage or give it away like a cash prize on *Family Feud*. All the government can do—and should do—is affirm the natural reality of the situation.

If marriage is anything, then it is an institution meant to bind a husband to his wife, a wife to her husband, and both mother and father to their children. If it is something at all, then it is that.

It is that or it is nothing. It is that or it is what people say it is now: just a temporary and soluble agreement between two people who feel some sort of mutual attraction. And if that's all it is, then certainly the government shouldn't acknowledge it or say anything about it one way or another.

Why do we need governments and courts to involve

themselves in creating laws and tax codes for some provisional alliance between two (or three, or 189) adults (or an adult and a child, or an adult and a barnyard animal) who merely wish to live together (or apart, or whatever they want) and "love" each other?

You see, if gay marriage is even possible—if marriage can fundamentally be an institution that includes same-sex partnerships—then it is, by definition, not solid enough or essential enough to our civilization to warrant legal challenges and Supreme Court cases. If "gay marriage" is equal to "traditional marriage," then they're both utterly pointless, unimportant, and not deserving of recognition by the government or courts.

You want to love another person? Go. Go love them. Go love the whole world. Nothing was ever stopping you. There was never any law preventing it. If marriage is only a loving bond between two (or however many) lovers, why would anyone ask for it to be legalized? That's not illegal, it never was, and it never could have been.

The very fact that we are having this conversation proves that everyone involved sees marriage as something greater than a contract between consenting, loving adults. And if it's something more significant, then we are back to the old definition, which is the only definition that makes sense in the first place.

In the end, it turns out, you can't argue for gay marriage without arguing against it.

7

Acceptance Is Mandatory

WHY IT'S ALWAYS A MISTAKE TO APPEASE
THE LIBERAL RODENT

There is a fable dating back to ancient times called *If You Give a Mouse a Cookie*. It tells the story of a psychotic rodent who barges into a young boy's house and demands a delicious baked good. Once he's devoured the treat, he demands some milk, then a straw, then a napkin, and before long he's consumed everything in the house, including the house itself, and the poor boy dies alone in the cold. That's how the story was told to me, anyway.

Keen political observers have noticed that the American Left is much like the domineering household pest in this tale. It is never finished eating. Make one compromise with it, and immediately it will want another.

Concede any ground, and soon it will stake its claim on the ground to which you just retreated. Give it an inch and it will take your soul.

Conservatives were too slow to understand this reality, and too fearful to do anything about it once they came to understand it, so now the progressive march to forcibly eradicate opposing opinions is in full swing. It was not enough for progressivism to become the predominant ideology in our culture; it was not enough for it to commandeer the media, Hollywood, the educational system, government, and the corporate world; it was not enough for progressivism to, for all intents and purposes, win the argument. Now it must be the only argument.

On the matter of gay marriage, as I've laid out over the course of the last two chapters, progressives achieved historic power to enshrine and codify into law the fantastical "right to gay marriage." More consequentially, they won the battle of public opinion. Their premise on this issue became the premise of our entire culture.

If liberalism were an ideological force determined to convert the masses through argument and activism, it would now consider itself victorious, and begin the less exciting task of maintaining and sustaining the "advances." But liberalism, or progressivism, is exactly what it claims to be. It must keep moving. It must tear down walls it already tore down and vanquish enemies who've long since surrendered. Because it is not anchored in truth, it is not anchored at all. It cannot stay still and defend this New World it created, because it's not the creation of something new that it's interested in, but the destruction of something old. Progressivism is an ideology of *anti*'s. It hates everything that the old Christian civilization built, not because it believes it can build something better, but because it hates that anything was built at all.

For this reason, it cannot rest on its laurels and let the matter of marriage be. Its next project, which has been in motion for some time now, is to punish, censor, and criminalize the few holdouts in the "traditional marriage" camp. This ends, make no mistake, with shuttered churches and noncompliant pastors in prison. I'm not saying we'll all be attending church services in the catacombs next week (I wouldn't know where to find a suitable catacomb anyway), but we are not immune to the fate so many Christians in other nations have suffered.

Christian persecution is not something confined only to history books and Middle Eastern hellholes. Once we became a post-Christian society, it was inevitable that we'd become an anti-Christian society.

A CREEPING TYRANNY

We've already seen, since about 2012, a sharp escalation in the Left's war on the First Amendment rights of Christians.

It started with the small private companies in, or tangentially connected to, the wedding industry. Like something out of a George Orwell acid trip, bakers and photographers and other merchants who might sometimes provide goods and services for wedding ceremonies found themselves forced by law to bake or take pictures or perform whatever other service for homosexuals. A few examples you might remember from over the past few years:

- A baker in Colorado was found guilty of human rights violations because he declined to bake a cake for a gay couple's wedding. The baker, Jack Phillips, specifically targeted by this attention-seeking couple, initially declined to make a cake for the gay wedding because he had deep and profound religious objections to the ceremony. This left the gay couple with two options: (1) Go, like, find any other baker in the area. (2) Try to legally force the man to bake the cake, because, you know, freedom.

  Of course, as usual, they went with option two. And, as in every similar case across the country, the offending businessman made clear that he was perfectly willing to serve homosexuals—he just couldn't lend his services to an *activity* he finds morally objectionable.

  But it didn't matter. His case made it all the

way to the Colorado Court of Appeals, where the findings of a state commission were upheld. CNN reported that in 2014 the Colorado Civil Rights Commission ruled that "Phillips must create cakes for same-sex celebrations, re-train his staff, and file quarterly reports for two years to confirm the bakery wasn't turning away customers because they were gay or lesbian."

- A florist in Washington State faced penalties for not providing flowers for a gay wedding. The Christian grandmother was fined $1,000 and ordered to pay the legal fees of the gay couple whose human rights she violated by not providing the lilies and roses they demanded. She was instructed to work gay weddings in the future, making her and the other businesspeople in her boat into glorified indentured servants.

- The New Mexico Supreme Court found that a small photography company in the state is not allowed to decide which weddings it will photograph and which weddings it won't photograph. The court compelled the Christian photographers who own the business to work gay weddings, despite their religious convictions.

This ruling came after the owner, Elaine Huguenin, politely declined to photograph a lesbian wedding back in 2006. As Huguenin explained: they will "gladly serve gays and lesbians—by, for example, providing them with portrait photography—whenever doing so would not require them to create expression conveying messages that conflict with their religious beliefs."

But this wasn't good enough. Even though the lesbian customers promptly found a different photographer who charged better rates, they still took the matter to the courts.

- A bakery in Oregon was fined over $135,000 for not servicing a gay wedding. The labor commissioner awarded the damages to a lesbian couple who claim they were emotionally devastated and distraught when they were forced to go to one of the dozens of other bakeries or grocery stores within a few-mile radius.

- A Catholic company in Albany, New York, was charged with civil rights violations when it refused to host a gay wedding on its farm. The company was forced to pay $10,000 to the state, and another $3,000 to help heal the "mental pain and suffering" it inflicted on the aggrieved lesbians.

- A T-shirt company in Kentucky found itself embroiled in a legal battle for committing the crime of refusing to make T-shirts for a gay pride parade in Lexington. The owner, again, referred the parade organizers to other T-shirt companies that offer the same service for the same price. But, again, that wasn't good enough. The owner was charged with human rights violations, as the case bounced around to different courts, eventually getting tossed out on appeal. All of this because a guy didn't want to make T-shirts.

And, though not instances of governmental intrusions, gay fascists have, in their single-minded pursuit of ideological conformity, also set their sights on Catholic priests who follow Church law; fast-food restaurants whose owners haven't pledged allegiance to their cause; Christian hosts on HGTV who talk about the Bible sometimes; football commentators who don't properly worship at the altar of a gay defensive end from Missouri; reality stars who talk about the Bible sometimes; tech CEOs who donate to legislation protecting traditional marriage; and many, many others.

In all of these cases, offenders have been threatened, blackmailed, bullied, boycotted, fired, or legally punished for, in the minds of the gay mob, "discriminating."

FREEDOM OF ASSOCIATION FOR ME, BUT NOT FOR THEE

In each of these cases, not a single gay person was singled out, victimized, persecuted, or otherwise preyed upon for being gay. The bakers and bridal shop owners and florists and T-shirt companies and photographers never once "refused service to gay people." They refused to participate in activities involving gay people, but they never said, "You are gay so you may not purchase a cupcake in my establishment." Why would they do that, anyway? The act of serving a delicious pastry to a homosexual is not, by any Christian teaching I've ever heard, intrinsically immoral. *Nobody* is refusing service to gays just because they're gay. That's not the point. That's not what's happening.

We are only talking about people who, for religious reasons, opted not to play an *active role* in a gay wedding ceremony or gay pride festival. And, on the other side of that coin, we're talking about gays who wish to force private individuals to play that role, whether they like it or not.

The irony, of course, is that the effort to punish businesses who'd rather not associate with a gay wedding undermines one of the central arguments used to legally justify the gay wedding in the first place. After all, if a man has the right to choose whom he marries, a business owner surely must have the right to choose whom he serves.

A gay wedding is, supposedly, a victory for freedom of association. Yet gay activists see no problem with forcing Christians to associate with it. Freedom of association is not a terribly strong argument for gay marriage, but it is the strongest argument. Really, it's the only argument. "Let us associate with each other however we want. We are consenting adults."

I don't think consent should be the single criterion for making something legal, as if everything is OK so long as all the people involved in it want to be involved in it, but if that is your position, there is no possible way to exclude the butcher, the baker, and the candlestick-maker from that principle. Until rabid Christians show up uninvited to gay weddings to see to it that *nobody* provides cakes and photography, they cannot be said to be depriving homosexuals of anything. They are merely choosing not to associate themselves with the event. They are choosing not to consent.

Be that as it may, it's now clear that some people have freedom of association and some don't, just as some have freedom of religion and, with each passing year, more and more don't. It should have been obvious when they first came after the bakers and photographers that the churches and religious organizations would be next.

A LOGICAL CONCLUSION

If the government can force a caterer to cater a gay wedding, and a photographer to photograph a gay wedding, and a baker to bake for a gay wedding, why can't it force a church to conduct a gay wedding? Why, precisely? Because the church is a "religious institution"? So what? Where is it written that only religious institutions have a right to religious expression? I know where that distinction certainly isn't made: the Constitution. If a photographer does not have the freedom to express his religious beliefs on the job, why should he have it just because he walks into a church? If bakers, and photographers, and T-shirt printers can be compelled to abandon their opposition to gay marriage, why can't pastors?

But when we lost the argument against gay marriage, we lost the argument for our own religious liberty. The two happened at once, as we are beginning to see. Indeed, as liberals breathlessly argued, a church should not be allowed to keep slaves chained to the radiators in the basement just because some bizarre sect believes that slavery is divinely prescribed. Moreover, a pastor in this fictional denomination should not be allowed to rile his congregants into a frenzy and command them to go out and take slaves of their own. You cannot commit human rights violations, no matter your religion, and you cannot intentionally provoke others to do the same.

I agree with this sentiment. Religion cannot be used as a cover for atrocities, and it cannot be used as a vehicle to actively entice others into committing atrocities. A pastor may find the new Seth Rogen film objectionable (who doesn't?), but he can't call on his flock to burn their local theater to the ground and take Rogen hostage until he promises to stop producing movies (which would be a favorable outcome, although achieved through questionable means).

The only real question, then, is whether gay marriage actually is a human right. The answer to that question is no, of course, but anyone who answers yes must logically believe, or will soon logically believe, that any attempts by anyone to infringe on this right should be prevented and punished.

The groundwork has clearly been laid for a move against churches and other explicitly religious organizations. Really, it had already been set before that by the Obamacare contraception mandate, which, though not related to gay marriage, empowered the government to force private companies, Christian schools, and even nuns to pay for birth control pills and abortifacients. Different parts of the mandate were challenged and struck down by the courts, but the precedent had been set: your beliefs will not be respected if they are not consistent with the mainstream wisdom of the age.

In 2016, finally, the move to impose tolerance of gay marriage on the churches and the religious community began in earnest. Early in the year, a religious liberty bill passed through Georgia's house and senate aroused the ire of the entire country, prompting the courageous governor, Nathan Deal, to veto the legislation. Caving to intense pressure from Disney, Time Warner, Starz, the Weinstein Company, AMC, Viacom, Marvel, CBS, MGM, NBC, the NFL, Coca-Cola, Apple, and many other companies, Deal tossed the bill into the garbage on the grounds that it was discriminatory against gays.

Despite this inordinate reaction, the horrific bill they were all so angry about would have simply accomplished the following:

- Protect a pastor from being forced to perform a gay wedding against his will.
- Protect religious organizations from being forced to host gay weddings against their will.
- Protect religious organizations from being forced to hire someone who opposes their fundamental tenets, beliefs, and goals.

Liberals opposed granting very basic religious protections to religious organizations. It was only a few months prior to the Georgia controversy that leftists were still insisting that *only* religious organizations should have religious rights. When the country debated a similar law in Indiana or any of those various cases involving bakers and photographers and so on, liberals said over and over again that *if* the companies in question were conspicuously and officially "religious," they wouldn't have a problem with gays being "discriminated against" on religious grounds.

There is no coherent constitutional argument you could make against a bill that protects the right of a religious group to be a religious group, unless the religious group is essentially reclassified as a hate group, which is the ultimate goal. In no universe would it make sense to claim that a man has a right to use the facilities of, or be employed by, an organization whose fundamental tenets he actively opposes and defies, unless his being gay endows him with that special and extraordinary right, which is the argument liberals have already successfully made and had codified by the Supreme Court.

THE RIGHT TO DISCRIMINATE

To make this broadly a matter of "discrimination" is absurd. If a church, Christian school, or pastor does have the constitutional right to the free exercise of religion, then they must have the right to discriminate. Exercising your religion means abiding by the moral doctrines of your religion, and a moral doctrine by its very nature excludes and discriminates against activities it deems immoral. So the right to the free exercise of religion, if it exists at all, *does absolutely guarantee "the right to discriminate."* If it does not, then there is no freedom of religion. And, if you're keeping up, you know that's the whole point: there is no longer true freedom of religion in America. Not anymore.

Discriminate: "to make a distinction in favor of or against a person or thing on the basis of the group, class, or category to which the person or thing belongs"; "show partiality"; "to note or observe a difference"; "to distinguish"; "to differentiate."

When you choose not to partake in a gay wedding, you are making a distinction against it based on the category to which it belongs. You are showing partiality. You are observing a difference. You are distinguishing. You are differentiating. You are *discriminating*. And so what?

There is no universal right to not be discriminated against. I realize that we have invented this right, but it does not actually exist as a constitutional or moral reality. To say that we have the right to be free from discrimination is to say that no individual can ever make a distinction in favor of or against us or our actions based on group, class, or category. This is ludicrous on its face. We all engage in this sort of discrimination on a daily basis. We all decide whom to associate with, and in what manner, and to what degree, and in what form, based on, yes, discrimination. Whether positive or negative, critical or complimentary, we discriminate—make distinctions, decide for or against—all the time. It's part of being human.

If your daughter comes home with her bedraggled sixty-eight-year-old serial sex offender boyfriend and you react somewhat suspiciously to this arrangement, you have discriminated. If a man wearing a ski mask and toting a chain saw shows up to your door at 3:00 a.m. and asks to borrow a cup of sugar, you have discriminated if you shut the door in a hurry and call the cops. If you chose to wear a blue shirt today rather than a brown shirt, you discriminated. If you made a choice between one thing and another, if you drew conclusions based on available evidence, if you rejected anyone or anything for any reason, you discriminated.

How could an individual possess the absolute right to be free from distinctions and differentiations? What does that mean? Where does this right come from? Certainly not God, seeing as how He bestowed on us the mental facilities to discern, which is another synonym for discriminate.

Certainly not from the law, given that the law is the Constitution, and the Constitution specifically protects the right to discriminate in the very first amendment to the Bill of Rights. So this is a "right" rooted in nothing more than the whims of pandering politicians. Now, we certainly have the right to be free from unfair or prejudicial treatment by the government. But that's not what we're talking about here. These photography businesses and wedding venues aren't run by the State; they're run by people, and those people do all sorts of discerning over whom they do business with and the manner in which they do it. It would be rather impossible to run any sort of successful enterprise otherwise.

Let's look at this another way. The right to discriminate—that is, the right of a private individual to make decisions in favor of or against another individual or activity—is an active right. It protects my ability to do and say things. It protects, or it is supposed to protect, my power to exercise agency over myself, my property, and my business. That is the nature of a human right, and human rights are elemental principles that speak to our inherent dignity and worth as rational beings. That's why the Declaration of Independence outlines "life, liberty, and the pursuit of happiness," proposing that all people should be granted these things, because we are entitled to them by the very nature of our humanity.

I can see, then, how agency over my property and my business can be called a human right. Without that agency, I am deprived of that which makes me human. This all makes sense. It's coherent. It's consistent. It might, in practice, lead to hurt feelings and—horror of horrors—it might force a gay person to Google for another of the twelve thousand bridal shops in her geographic vicinity, but the fact that it poses a possible inconvenience to another person does not undo the right itself.

So how does the right to not be discriminated against factor in? When the T-shirt company or wedding venue or photographer or baker or candlestick-maker declines to do business with us, which of our human rights have been infringed on? The right to access baked goods? What's the underlying liberty we're trying to protect? When someone murders you, they haven't infringed on your right to not be murdered; they've infringed on your underlying right to life. What, then, is the liberty at the foundation in this case? The right to a product or service made or provided by another person? Well, if we have that right, when does it develop and where does it end? Are we all suddenly bequeathed with the inalienable right to affordable wedding photography the moment Susie Q down the street decides to open her own freelance business? Do we have this right even before she opens? Is she compelled by some mysterious cosmic force to become a photographer so as to fulfill society's entitlement to her photography services?

And if we have a right to the photography, how can she even justify charging for it?

Does she own her business or not? If we are entitled to it, I suppose she doesn't. Should she run all of her business decisions by us? How does that work? Should she hire Gallup and conduct a national poll of some sort? Certainly it goes without saying that if you ask her to come snap a few pics at your next orgy or Klan meeting, she must absolutely oblige. To refuse would be, by every definition, discrimination, and that would infringe on your right to not be discriminated against.

The people who want to legally prevent religions from "discriminating" against homosexuals really want to destroy Christianity. As I've demonstrated, their stance cannot be based on a general opposition to all forms of discrimination. If they actually believe that gay marriage is a human right, then their only recourse is to rid the nation of the Christian scourge.

When it comes down to it, they do not believe that certain religions, in their current forms, should be given safe harbor anywhere within our borders. They could pretend otherwise back when they were "only" trying to strip rights from private, secular companies, but now that they're passionately opposing the rights of religious groups to abide by their own religions, the charade is over. They want to abolish Christianity and the only real question left is how, exactly, they plan to do it.

I didn't quite expect our culture to make the transition from "only religious groups can be religious" to "every church must have its religious beliefs sanctioned by the government" so quickly, but I knew it was inevitable. This is why you cannot compromise with leftists or cede your position based on their arguments. They do not want to come to an understanding—they want obedience. That's all they will accept. Make one concession and they'll demand another, and another, and another, unto infinity. If you let up on the rightness of your fundamental position—in this case, that homosexuality is a perversion and gay marriage is an abomination—then you'll quickly discover that you've let up on your right to hold that position.

I suspect the next step will be the revocation of tax-exempt status for religious entities that do not amend their doctrines to make sodomy and same-sex "marriage" morally righteous. Churches and religious organizations who do not strike Romans 1:26–28, Jude 1:5–8, 1 Timothy 1:8–11, Mark 10:6–9, 1 Corinthians 7:2, and many other passages from the Bible will be subject to financial and tax penalties that will cripple most of them.

Once that is complete, the full, Roman-style persecution will begin in earnest. If there will be any silver lining when that day arrives, it will be final separation of the wheat from the chaff. I suspect we'll discover quite a lot of chaff. But the few Christians who remain steadfast in their faith, even as it is outlawed and its adherents subjected to all manner of indignities, can at least look around at one another and know they are finally in the company of true believers.

8

The Insanity of Transgenderism

HOW A MINUSCULE MINORITY
BENT THE CULTURE
TO ITS WILL

The world is going insane, and I don't mean it's going insane in some figurative sense. I mean it's actually, really, literally losing its mind. To be insane is to be unable to distinguish between fantasy and truth, to lose one's grip on reality. That is our cultural condition. If an entire society could be wrapped in a straitjacket and thrown into a padded room, ours would be a candidate. And perhaps there is no greater expression of this collective lunacy than our devolving understanding of gender.

As we've seen, progressives are on a mission to radically and fundamentally redefine the essential pillars of human civilization. We've discussed their efforts to redefine human life through abortion and euthanasia and to redefine marriage and family through the mandated acceptance of homosexuality, and now we turn to their war on gender. This assault is taking place on two fronts, advanced by two terrible "isms": "transgenderism" and feminism.

Ironically, as we'll examine, these two "isms" are in direct competition with each other, even if their proponents don't realize it. We'll talk about feminism and its campaign against the beautiful and complementary nature of the sexes later, but first we have to deal with "transgenderism." As a side note, I put quotes around "transgenderism" because it's a made-up word denoting a made-up concept. The prefix *trans-* means "beyond or through," and nobody is *beyond* gender. Our gender *is* binary. Once again, progressives have come up with a word that implicitly confirms their point and convinced us all to use it even as we contest that very point. Brilliant. But for the sake of simplicity, I will be using the made-up word here, and I will not always put the sarcastic quotes around it. I leave it to you to fill those in every time it comes up.

A SMALL BUT POWERFUL FORCE

It's necessary to deal with transgenderism first because, for one thing, nobody else will. There are some conservative and Christian voices out there willing to articulate our case when it comes to the sanctity of life, and there are some, but fewer, who will speak up on marriage, but it seems almost nobody will whisper a word of protest when the conversation turns to transgenderism. There's a lot of awkward silence and submissive nodding and, worse, celebratory applause, but only the softest, smallest, most scattered protest.

Those of us who will protest increasingly feel like the child in the famous parable, shouting that the emperor has no clothes. Only, in this instance, I suppose the emperor *is* wearing clothes—it's just that he bought them in the women's section.

Apart from the random uncooperative subject who can't yet bring himself to play along, everyone else seems to have surrendered without much of a struggle. We fought—some of us, anyway—when they came to redefine life and marriage, but I guess by the time they made it to gender we were too exhausted to resist. *Fine, whatever, you can have it*, we all said with a sigh.

Of course, our apathy and cowardice could be partly explained by the absolute viciousness with which the homosexual and transgender lobby defends its lies. And, speaking as someone who's been on the receiving end of said viciousness on a number of occasions, I can attest that to call them vicious is an understatement.

It's really a remarkable thing when you think about

it. Our culture is so dominated and controlled by—numerically speaking—one of the most insignificant groups on the planet. Homosexuals are already a relatively rare breed, and transgenders are even scarcer. There are a handful of gender-confused people in this country, but their demands and desires defeat everyone else's, without exception. If you're a woman and a man in a dress wants to join you in the ladies' room, you must invite him in with a smile.

This is the power they wield, and it's why so many of us are reluctant to oppose them—but it's also why we must.

Why do they wield this kind of power? Why has our culture bowed in trembling capitulation and submitted itself to the fantastical claims of a microscopically small number of cross-dressing fetishists? I think there are two reasons.

First, very simply, our progressives have no more dragons to slay. Progressivism, having run out of battlegrounds, now plunges itself right into a moral and intellectual abyss. It has nothing else to say—it's already made its point many times over—but because it is, at its core, a deception, it cannot remain still. It must "progress," in that it must always run left, even when it appears to have run out of room.

Compare this with Christianity, for example. Traditional Christians have been making the same points, taking the same stands, saying the same things, teaching the same moral lessons, and fighting for the same values and the same truths for two thousand years. Christianity is immovable because it is eternal. Christianity does not invent new causes, because its one and only cause has always been truth, and truth never changes. While the liberalism of today sounds significantly different from the liberalism of six years ago, the Christianity of today sounds exactly the same as the Christianity of six hundred years ago or a thousand years ago. Christians must defend the truth against new attacks, but the truth itself, that which is being defended, remains steady, present, and alive.

Liberalism has no truth at its foundation, so it can only keep moving. Christians live in a house built on rock, but secular progressives have no house at all. They are ideological nomads, wandering ever farther into the ether. In other words, they look to dissolve the concept of gender because, well, what else is there to do?

A MENTAL ILLNESS BY ANY OTHER NAME

But secondly, to understand the most important *why*, we must understand the *what*. According to the people who come up with these things, a transgender person is someone who does not "identify" as their physical sex. The dictionary tells me that the word *transgender* "denotes a person whose self-identity does not conform unambiguously to conventional notions of male or female gender." That sounds like a load of unadulterated, grade A, 93 percent lean nonsense, and it is, but it's also true that people can suffer from obsessive delusions about their bodies. This is called body dysmorphia, which lies at the root of anorexia and other disorders. A man who feels distressed by his own penis—who feels like his reproductive organs shouldn't be there, or should be functionally different—probably falls under this umbrella. But the mental health community has come up with a different category to describe transgenders.

Until recently, someone with gender confusion would have been diagnosed with gender identity disorder (GID). GID applies to anyone who experiences a conflict between their physical gender and the gender they "identify with." Progressives, however, took exception to this medical diagnosis because—to their perpetual shock and horror—it seemed to imply that the subject had a disorder. GID put the emphasis on the subject's muddled self-image, trying to help them align their perception with reality.

This is terribly offensive. How dare a psychologist insinuate that a man who thinks he's a woman is actually still a man? How dare he try to treat the man's mind as sick, rather than his body? Much as they did in 1973, when homosexual activists forced the American

Psychiatric Association to remove homosexuality from its *Diagnostic and Statistical Manual of Mental Disorders*, the LGBT cabal again sprang into action, pressuring the nation's psychiatrists to end their heinous habit of practicing psychiatry. Ultimately, and yet again for political reasons, the *DSM* was changed to reflect the politically correct inclinations of our time.

Now GID is gone and in its place is "gender dysphoria," a condition—don't call it a mental illness!—that treats the subject's feelings, not their disordered identity, as the problem. The issue isn't that a man thinks he should have a vagina; it's that he feels bad about not having one. Don't worry, that doesn't mean his feelings should change to concur with his body. It's the other way around, obviously. To "treat" these feelings, a doctor can prescribe hormone pills and cosmetic mutilation to align his body to his feelings.

And we're not just talking about adults. Indeed, if your four-year-old son rifles through the box of costumes and pulls out a sparkly pink princess dress, the medical community will view that as a potential symptom of his latent gender dysphoria. You see, that's not a young boy being silly and curious. No, that's a young boy discovering his inner female self. That wasn't a dress he found in the box—it was his soul! These days, a few more incidents like that might be enough to convince a doctor, and some particularly progressive parents, to begin "transitioning" the child into a lifetime of bewildering confusion and silent, crippling anguish.

There have been many recent public cases of a prepubescent child—usually a boy—being diagnosed as gender dysphoric and placed on hormone pills, thereby stunting his growth, delaying puberty, and destroying any chance he had of growing into a normal, healthy young man.

In Minnesota—a beautiful state filled with maniacs— the parents of a five-year-old boy recently sued their son's charter school, claiming he was discriminated against because, they say, the young boy discovered that he was actually a girl, and when he came to kindergarten dressed as a girl, the other students pointed and laughed. The parents took legal action because they claim that the kindergarten class should be teaching the little kids about gender identity and that, at the ages of four and five, the children should already be sufficiently indoctrinated so as not to even look sideways at one of their classmates dressing in drag.

BULLYING IS NOT THE PROBLEM

I must make a note here that might get me into trouble. We hear that transgenders like this poor, abused boy are "bullied." The other kids snicker at them and say unkind things and so forth. We're told that this is a troubling sign about our youth. But I would suggest that the opposite might be the case. I submit that it is much more dangerous to live in a culture in which kids are not laughing at a boy dressed in girls' clothes.

After all, there are only two reasons why a kid would refrain from pointing and giggling at a cross-dresser. One, perhaps the kid is very mature, very gentle, very kind, very well behaved. This is a good reason. If that's why they don't "bully," I say that's wonderful. And that, of course, is how we should train our kids. When my kids point or laugh at anyone, for any reason, I discipline them.

But if kids are not openly treating a bizarre and unnatural thing as bizarre and unnatural, it's likely not because they are mature but because they do not *recognize* it as bizarre and unnatural. So, while bullying is a terrible thing, it comes, in this case, from an innate understanding that something is disordered, weird, and ridiculous. It's good to put a stop to bullying by teaching compassion, but it's bad to put a stop to bullying by teaching falsehoods. And it is most certainly a falsehood that a boy in girls' clothes is normal, good, and healthy.

The real issue for transgenders is not how others feel about them but how they feel about themselves. The transgender self-identity so often leads to self-hatred, or you might say that self-hatred is what leads to the transgender self-identity. As is often cited by the LGBT camp, the suicide rate among transgenders is tragically high. Most studies indicate that a full 40 percent of gender-confused individuals attempt suicide. This is ten times higher than the rate among the general population. *Ten times.* Gay activists tell us that gender-confused people are subjected to the aforementioned bullying, which, they say, explains the suicides and suicide attempts. High rates of bullying allegedly *correlate* with high rates of suicide, so they assume that one must *cause* the other.

Now, I don't doubt that transgenders are bullied, and I certainly condemn the bullying of anyone for any reason. I also don't doubt that transgender kids sometimes complain of being tormented in school before taking their own lives. This is a horrible thing, without question.

But does bullying explain why the rate of suicide attempts is *one thousand percent higher* among transgenders? Bullying is a common problem, unfortunately. Very few children will make it through twelve or thirteen years of grade school without being subjected to an extraordinary onslaught of teasing and insults, yet the bullied transgender is far, far more likely to resort to suicide than the bullied non-transgender. Why?

Further, if external factors are to blame for the transgender suicide epidemic, why does the rate remain sky-high regardless of the external factors? If X (bullying) creates Y (transgender suicide), shouldn't there be less of Y if X is less common? Yet that isn't how it works. The transgender suicide rate remains nearly constant no matter the circumstances, even in tolerant, über-liberal places like Sweden.

The LGBT camp has never shown that the suicide rate is demonstrably lower in more "accepting" environments, because it can't show any such thing. Trans folks are at a high risk for self-harm no matter where they are, no matter how old, no matter if they grow up in an especially progressive place or some backward Christian cesspool down south.

Even after completing gender reassignment, the gender-confused are still much more likely to resort to suicide. This, again, makes no sense, according to liberal orthodoxy. If they are able to become their "true selves," the disparity in suicides should disappear, but it doesn't.

Moreover, the link between nonacceptance and suicide doesn't hold up when you look at other groups. For instance, suicide rates among black children are up over the past few decades, even though I think we'd all agree that blacks suffered worse persecution in the past than they do today.

It's clear that transgender people are unhappy, regardless of their circumstance, their environment, or how far along they are in their transitioning process.

This is a crucial point, because it shows that progressive ideas benefit no one, and often do the most damage to the groups they're designed to cater to. Another devastating example of this is the astronomically high suicide rate among post-abortive women. A woman who gets an abortion is six hundred times more likely to kill herself than a woman who gives birth. Again, progressives will punt the responsibility for this staggering figure over to the other side, claiming that these women commit suicide because pro-lifers make them feel guilty and so on, but an honest person must recognize that there is something deeper at play here. When people live by the secular progressive values of our culture, all they find is misery and despair.

THE PRIMACY OF EMOTIONS

Why does our culture contort itself to justify and accommodate something that is so desperately absurd and so egregiously harmful to everyone involved?

Because transgenderism puts feelings above all. In a world where a person can reject his biology in favor of his lust and his emotions, the individual reigns supreme. My self-identity trumps my actual identity. Reality becomes subservient to desire. This is the key. It is, more than any other reason, why our culture has taken up the transgender banner and fights so ruthlessly to protect it. In transgenderism, man achieves his final victory over truth and truth's God.

No longer do we declare with confidence, "I am . . ." We don't want to be so confined and pigeonholed. Instead we say, "I identify as . . ." What we identify with has taken the place of what we are. In the process, all forms of identity—every delineation and distinction that defines us and distinguishes us from everyone else—have begun to disintegrate.

When you understand the motivations behind the advancement of transgender propaganda, you start to understand why many progressives never mentioned a word about transgenderism up until the past couple of years. When, for instance, Barack Obama launched his unilateral campaign to rid our society of the archaic, oppressive policy of sex segregation in public school restrooms, many wondered why, if he thought transgenders were the victims of Jim Crow–style persecutions, he never said much about them until a few months before his second term expired.

The answer is that neither Obama nor most other progressives over the age of twenty-three actually believe that a man can be a woman if he feels like one. If they did believe something so fantastical as that, it probably would have come up at some point before just now. But these are, despite appearances, largely intelligent and mentally competent people. They know full well that their sex ed teachers weren't telling fibs decades ago when they taught the now-controversial theory that men have penises.

They realize that transgenderism is science fiction. It is the sort of belief that cult leaders don't tell the new converts about until they've been sufficiently brain-washed for many rigorous months. It's why the Church of Scientology doesn't speak openly about the galactic Lord Xenu, who, according to Scientologist theology, stored the souls of seventy-five billion humans in giant volcanoes (or something like that). This is the really severe stuff. The stuff that the cult leaders themselves don't believe, which is what makes them the leaders and not the disciples.

But progressives in the older generations have adopted transgenderism as their latest cause because it is, for them, a vehicle. It is a delivery system for all of the things we've talked about in this book—relativism, secularism, the destruction of Christianity. Make identity itself relative and you will have finally and totally divorced yourself from reality and all of the moral and scientific laws that come with it. That's what progressives get out of trans-genderism. The fact that transgenderism is utter baloney is irrelevant to them.

IT'S A TRANSWORLD

That explains why liberalism has begun to unironically adopt other forms of "trans" identities, such as transracialism, the idea that a white woman might legitimately identify as a black woman, or that a white man ought to be taken seriously when he says he identifies as a Chinese lesbian. Transgender. Transrace. Throw it all in. You can't pick one and leave the others.

Then there's transspecies, which isn't just a concept hilariously invented by *South Park*. There exists an actual community of people who pretend to be animals and call themselves "otherkins." As a piece in *Vice* once put it, "Otherkins are people too; they just identify as nonhuman." A lot of liberals take these bestial fetishists seriously. They have to, I guess.

Transgender. Transrace. Transspecies. These are different brands of crazy, but they are all fundamentally the same—100 percent comparable, right down the line—and we are witnessing the mainstreaming of them all.

And it doesn't stop there. You may have heard of the small but vibrant "transabled" community. These are people who feel certain they were supposed to be born legless, armless, deaf, paralyzed, or crippled in some other way. Eventually, if they aren't given rigorous psychological treatment, they often resort to disfiguring themselves to achieve the realization of their "true selves." Recently, the world met Jewel Shuping, a woman who was so certain she was meant to be blind that she had her psychologist pour drain cleaner into her eyes.

The LGBT cabal has so far rejected transabled minorities—no doubt realizing that a guy who wants his arm cut off is a little too uncomfortably similar to a guy who wants his penis cut off—but soon they, too, will be welcomed. The transabled are the closest cousins—practically siblings—of transgenders. If a gender-confused woman should lop off her healthy breasts as a form of "treatment," why shouldn't a psychologist prescribe drain-cleaner eye droplets to a woman who fetishizes blindness? These situations are exactly analogous. The differences between them are merely cosmetic.

Transgender. Transrace. Transspecies. Transabled. Tolerance will be legally mandated for everyone. There is no stopping the trans-train at this point. All aboard. Soon a man will say he identifies as a legless female Siberian moose with dwarfism and we will be expected to applaud him and promptly provide public accommodations befitting a disabled moose. Soon we will all melt together into an amorphous muddle of ever-changing identity expressions. We will be like mounds of clay. Shape-shifters. Blobs of nondescript androgyny.

SELF-DEFEATING MESSAGES

But the most fascinating part of the transgender/trans-anything movement is how it so aggressively contradicts almost everything else progressives have said on the subject of gender. We've been told for years that "gender is a social construct," but transgender theory often conflicts directly with that idea. Progressives tell us that gender is a societal invention that imposes certain expectations of behavior and appearance on men and women. Society, we're informed, oppresses the human person by forcing it to act and look a certain way based solely on its anatomy.

Personally, I think these "gender roles" are often good, useful, and important—we'll get into that later—but even if I accepted their version of things, transgenderism would still be nonsensical. Perhaps *more* so.

In demolishing the gender "social construct," isn't the whole point to create a society where men can act in ways traditionally associated with women and where women can act in ways traditionally associated with men? If gender is indeed a social construct, then it seems the ultimate goal would be a culture where men can wear mascara and yoga pants and *still be considered men*. But progressives defeat their own point by next telling us that when a man acts like a woman, he actually *is* one, which is odd considering they just got through telling us there's no such thing as "acting like a woman."

They went from insisting that "social constructs" prevent men from wearing bras to insisting that if a man wears a bra he should promptly get himself a pair of breasts to go with it. They've not only reinforced gender stereotypes but given them a power not even the most ardent gender traditionalist would have ever conceived of.

Either men and women can defy these gender expectations, or they can't. But if defying the expectation is actually a medical symptom indicating that a person might be of the other gender, then he or she can't defy gender expectations. Progressives tell us in one breath that it's OK for boys to like pink and girls to like blue, and that we should stop expecting our sons to play sports and our daughters to play with dolls. These are just social norms, they say. We should not subscribe to such archaic notions. But suddenly they proceed to derail their own narrative when they next inform you that a girl liking blue and a boy playing with dolls might actually be a sign that the girl is a boy and the boy is a girl.

Wait. Are colors and toys and sports irrelevant things that have been arbitrarily assigned to certain genders by an oppressive society, or is the color pink so connected with the female identity that a female's aversion to it is an indication that she isn't really a female?

Who's really enforcing gender roles and social norms here? I'd say it's the people who call a girl transgender if she'd rather join a baseball league than the ballet.

One of the more well-known "transgender" children—only well known because her parents have chosen to make a mascot out of her—is a girl who now pretends to be a boy named Ryland. She "transitioned" at the age of five, after her parents decided that her confused and childish declarations about wanting to be a boy ought to be taken seriously. In various interviews, Ryland's parents—who ought to be charged and tried for felony child abuse—explain that they determined *she* is really a *he* because, among other things, she preferred not to wear girly outfits or have her bedroom walls painted pink.

In saner times, we may have just called the young girl a tomboy. Now we call her an Actual Boy. Her very early rejection of femininity was taken as evidence that she is not a female, sending the clear message that girls cannot reject femininity without rejecting their sex entirely. If anything "reinforces gender roles," I'd say this is it.

COMPETING "ISMS"

The competition between transgenderism and feminism is even more interesting. Feminists are the matriarchs of modern liberalism, and now they are watching as their movement suffers devastating and possibly fatal blows, not at the hands of conservative Christians but at the hands of men in dresses. Men are now barging their way into the female ranks and claiming not only membership but *headship*, and feminists are required to shut up and cooperate.

For years, feminists have contended that they can do everything as well as men can. Today, they must sit quietly while the gay lobby explains that, on the contrary, they can't even be women as well as men can. The mainstream acceptance of radical feminist theory has been, up until this point, one of liberalism's great achievements. And now it's all been compromised for the sake of a population that barely exists.

After all, according to mainstream feminist wisdom, there is no such thing as a "female brain" or a "female soul" or "feeling like a female." By the words of every liberal who has ever said anything on the subject of women's rights in the past four decades, how you dress, look, think, and feel have nothing to do with your womanhood. Usually it would be offensive and sexist to accuse a woman of acting like, thinking like, or feeling like a woman.

Feminism and transgenderism say two opposing things about what it means to be a woman. In fact, feminists have come up with the term *neurosexism* to condemn the misogynistic and "pseudoscientific" idea that male and female brains are different. But a man who calls himself transgender claims to have the brain of a female, so how does this work? Do you mean to tell me that the only people who can have female brains are males?

Meanwhile, feminists regularly insist that the absence of a uterus and a vagina excludes men from having an opinion about things like abortion. So a man can't have ideas about women's issues because he lacks the correct anatomy, but he can actually *be* a woman despite lacking the correct anatomy?

How does that make any kind of sense?

A DEGRADATION OF WOMANHOOD

For my part, I agree that a man can never lay claim to womanhood. I also agree that there is such a thing as a female brain and a female soul—and by extension female emotions and female personalities and female characteristics—but the trouble is that female brains and souls are always contained securely in female bodies. A man will never be born with a sloth's heart or a rhino's liver or a birch tree's root system, just as he will never be born with a woman's brain.

I'm told that white people appropriate black culture when they listen to Young Thug or wear flat-brimmed hats. I'm not sure such offenses constitute cultural theft as much as they indicate possible brain damage, but that's not the point. If we're worried about groups appropriating from other groups, I think we need to investigate the practice of calling a man a woman because he cuts off his genitals. If you look closely, you might find reason to consider this an appropriation of womanhood, or worse, a degradation of it.

There is more to being a woman than feminine facial features, Barbie dolls, and frilly underwear. Women are beautiful because they are women. Womanhood is itself beautiful. Women bring something distinct and special to the world. They fill a void and play a role that no man can.

A woman is a woman not merely because of whatever cosmetic feature a man might vaguely emulate. A woman is a woman because of her biology, which a man does not share and never will. A woman is a woman because of her capacity to create life and harbor it in her body until birth, which a man cannot do. A woman is a woman because of her soul, her mind, her perspective, her experiences, and her unique way of thinking, of loving, and of being—all things transgenders can only mimic.

A woman is a woman. She has earned that title. She pays for that title. She suffers with that title and gives life with that title and lives from conception until death and beyond with that title. She *is* that title. She should not be told that it's such a flimsy thing that a man with enough money can buy his way into it. It's demeaning and reductive, and as a father and a husband and a son and a brother, I take exception to it. I can only imagine what women might say if they were allowed to be open about it.

And notice I said I "can only imagine," because that's all I can do. I cannot experience a woman's thoughts or feelings due to the fact that I am not one. I can only be who I am. I am who I am, and that's all I'll ever be.

A BIBLICAL REBELLION

Here we see again how our culture's modern rebellion is really a biblical rebellion. Remember in Exodus when God said to Moses, "I AM WHO I AM"? I believe Popeye had a similar quote, but it should be noted that God said it first. In any case, God declared "I AM," not "I identify as your Lord today." He said "I AM" because He is. God exists. God *is* existence, God *is* reality. God is permanent, inexhaustible, unending. God *is* identity.

The origin of our own identity is found in God. The nearer we are to Him, the more we become ourselves. Today, we amputate ourselves from the source of identity and try to become our own source. God tells us to enter into the truth and find ourselves, but we have turned away from the truth and inward, into ourselves, collapsing into the void of the self separated from The Self.

The profound and beautiful truth is that we *are* ourselves, mind and body. Our bodies are not receptacles containing our souls. Our bodies and souls are one in harmony. Progressivism would have us believe that we can find true freedom—and our true selves—by rejecting our actual identities. But the aforementioned suicide rate of those who take this strategy to its extreme would seem to belie that notion. For a country that talks so incessantly about "self-acceptance," you'd think we'd understand that joy and peace can only be achieved once we've *accepted* our *selves*. I'm sure it's true that some people are born with mental derangements that make it difficult for them to see themselves for who they are. Others might be saddled with different psychological or spiritual afflictions that make them inclined to flee from themselves, claiming to be transgender or transspecies or transabled. We should treat these delusions, but we should not mistake them for insights. These people are who they are, no matter how they feel, just as you are who you are and I am who I am. That's the message we need to send.

It's a crucial lesson, yet I'm often urged to leave this whole issue alone and find something more important to talk about. There's no sense in arguing over identity expression and transgenderism and transwhateverism, I'm told. But you'll notice that only conservatives and Christians claim this to be an unimportant topic. While conservatives justify their miserable cowardice by insisting that it's just an irrelevant sideshow and that they're simply too wrapped up in more serious matters to pay it any mind, progressives continue to treat "transgenderism" as one of *the* most important cultural frontiers.

Any time a transgender person uses the bathroom

these days, progressives throw a parade like the Allies just defeated Germany. *Everyone* acts like it's a big deal. As long as they have the "correct" opinion, they're allowed to. And they're right—it *is* a big deal. If progressives can wield the power to demolish and remake even the definition of *man* and *woman* in their own ideological image, then they have achieved a *total and irreversible* cultural victory. They have reached into the universe and reshaped reality itself. They have become gods, or at least that's the kind of power we give them. You can blab on and on about economics and foreign policy, but if we live in a country where confusion, perversion, and self-worship reign supreme, what's the point? America will already be dead.

Progressivism has officially declared jihad upon reality. If our culture cooperates—if we relent and concede that science is relative and human beings are gods who can choose their own biological makeup, if the Left jumps over this shark and into the dark waters of full-fledged insanity, and if many in our society take the plunge right along with them—then there will be no stopping liberalism. The culture will be irretrievably lost.

If we willingly forfeit the definition of *man* and *woman*, right after forfeiting the definition of marriage, and long after forfeiting the definition of human life, then we will have no basis left to oppose anything else liberalism tries to do. We will have given it everything, ceded to its every demand, compromised on every single imaginable point, and that will be the end of it. All we'll be able to do, then, is sit and wait for our civilization to eat itself and collapse into dust.

We either draw a line here and make a final stand for objective truth—declaring without equivocation that some things, like our sex, are real and absolute—or else we give up and play along and tell ourselves that truth never mattered all that much anyway.

I have no real confidence that, as a culture, we'll choose truth. But if it's ever going to happen, now's the time. Liberals have made it clear that they intend to finally and categorically reject and outlaw reality itself. Now the question is: Will the rest of us stand up and do anything about it?

9

The Scourge of Feminism

HOW TURNING GENDER
INTO AN "ISM"
CREATES A FAUX PROBLEM

As we've discussed, the feminist movement and the LGBT movement cannot coincide indefinitely. One claims that women are superior, and the other claims that women do not, in any objective sense, exist. There is simply no way the Left can simultaneously advance both propositions. There is no way it can be a vehicle for feminist ideology and a vehicle for "men can have vaginas" ideology.

Indeed, transgenderism is the most anti-feminist phenomenon in history, even more so than Puritanism or Islam or Larry Flynt. But, until the glorious and inevitable day when the two factions decide to wage a mutually destructive war against each other, it's necessary that this book address and debunk both competing ideologies, as they both represent a leftist assault on gender.

Now, I will admit that my qualifications as a feminism expert are questionable at best. I haven't taken any feminist studies courses, nor have I ever used the word *gendered* in conversation, nor have I seen *The Vagina Monologues* nor any network drama from Shonda Rhimes, nor have I had any occasion to whip out femi-jargon like *phallogo-centrism* and *gynocriticism*. Worst of all, I'm a man. Still, I must endeavor to tackle the feminist problem if I want to offer a complete analysis of the Unholy Trinity.

Now, the general belief among most conservatives and anyone else who doesn't reside firmly on the leftmost end of the ideological spectrum is that "modern feminism" has its problems but that "true feminism" or "original feminism" or whatever qualifier you attach to it was quite useful in its day. Surveys show that most people do not identify themselves as feminists, and a large number have a negative opinion of the movement—shaped by college girls who screech about their safe spaces and accuse men of rape if they cast so much as a sideways glance in their general direction. But most people would likely say that feminism in its truest form is and has been a force for good. The movement was hijacked by ideological pirates at some point in the 1960s, conventional wisdom goes, and now it's become the monstrosity we all know and loathe today.

They're correct that the tone of feminism has grown more, shall we say, unpleasant, but I'm not sure that its present pettiness and ugliness is so much a perversion of its original design as a logical outgrowth of it. Perhaps it's fruitless to relitigate historical feminism, especially when the modern variety is so angry, destructive, and stupid by comparison. But to understand its anger, destructiveness, and stupidity, we must take a look at the ideas and philosophies at the foundation of the ideology.

In fact, before we get to the ideas, it might be said that the first problem with the ideology is that it's an ideology. Feminists of the first wave—Susan B. Anthony, Elizabeth Cady Stanton, Lucy Stone, etc.—built a new system of thought around a few worthy goals. The system was the problem, not the goals.

It was good that women won the right to vote and it was good that they achieved the right to participate more fully in society, but we've learned that a movement doesn't go away just because it's accomplished what it originally set out to do. It keeps lurching along, a cause in search of a reason. Think of it as a train still barreling forward even though the conductor and most of the original passengers have died or jumped overboard. And because the train now represents something popular and victorious, it quickly becomes a bandwagon for many of the sorts of people who were or would have been too afraid to jump on board back when it was still encountering resistance.

Eric Hoffer famously said, "Every great cause begins as a movement, becomes a business, and eventually degenerates into a racket." This is certainly the case with feminism, but it's worse because feminism is an ideology as well as a movement. Perhaps all movements are, to some extent, but feminism is all the more dangerous because it made gender into its own "ism."

The word feminism is derived from the French word *féminisme,* and in the grand scheme of things it's relatively new. You won't find the term used in any literature or publication until the early to mid–nineteenth century. The ism-izing (speaking of made-up words) of gender made sex and gender into a political issue, which has proven to be one of the most disastrous developments in human history. The early feminists may not have intended it, but they established something that would lead to over a century of death and division, with no end in sight.

Or maybe they did intend it. The truth is that feminism, from the very beginning, at its earliest stages, had a habit of presenting the family and religion as enemies of female equality. Elizabeth Cady Stanton, one of the godmothers of feminism, said that "the Bible and the Church have been the greatest stumbling blocks in the way of women's emancipation." This was a woman of the first wave—not the second, not the third. This is Scripture made out to be an obstacle, a "stumbling block," way down at the very foundation of feminist theory.

From the very beginning, at its earliest stages, feminism was an ideology with underpinnings of competition and exclusion. This oft-cited quote from Susan B. Anthony drives the point home: "There is not the woman born who desires to eat the bread of dependence, no matter whether it be from the hand of father, husband, or brother; for any one who does so eat her bread places herself in the power of the person from whom she takes it."

Casting "dependence" as the ultimate evil, characterizing the family and marriage as a power struggle—this goes to the very heart of feminist thought. It is the core of feminism, and every repugnant thing about the modern variety is rooted firmly in these ideas. Feminism may have been instrumental in accomplishing some very important goals, but those goals were achieved at the cost of legitimizing an ideology that encourages women to be resentful and suspicious of men.

UNORIGINAL IDEAS

Feminism may have brought about some necessary results a long time ago, but it was never necessary itself. The truthful insights of the old feminists—and they did have some truthful insights—were not uniquely feminist insights, but Christian insights. Whatever good existed in feminist philosophy was borrowed from Christian philosophy. No, Christian countries were not always fair to women, but that was due to their own failure to apply Christian principles universally. It was not a failure of the principles themselves.

What truth did feminism reveal that was not already known? That women are equal to men in human dignity and intrinsic value? No, feminism did not reveal this. Christianity revealed it. Christ revealed it. Christian thinkers throughout the ages have affirmed it and taught it, notably Thomas Aquinas, who said that women are meant to rule alongside men. That was over eight hundred years ago. Six hundred years before the term *feminist* existed, and over 750 years before the birth of modern feminist thought leaders like Amy Schumer and Kim Kardashian.

There's a pithy little slogan you often find plastered on T-shirts and bumper stickers and internet memes, originally coined by feminist writer Marie Shear, that defines feminism as "the radical notion that women are people." Most people would consider this to be the "core idea" of feminism, and therefore anyone who affirms the humanity of women must be a feminist, and anyone who disagrees with feminism must not think women are people.

Let's leave aside the irony that the only people in

America who literally deny the personhood of females—so long as the female resides in the womb—are feminists and focus on the absurdity and arrogance of this definition. Are we really supposed to believe that feminists were the first ones to realize that women are human beings? What did society consider them before—furniture? I might as well say that conservatism is the radical idea that oranges are fruit. Anyone who correctly places fruit on the food pyramid is a conservative. There, I just turned Bill Maher and Michael Moore into right-wingers (well, perhaps it's ambitious to assume that Michael Moore knows anything about fruit).

Jesus stopped the angry mob from stoning the adulterous woman to death two thousand years ago. He showed humanity and mercy to all people, especially women, and commanded His disciples to do the same. The Gospels did not send a message of female subjugation and dehumanization—far from it. Indeed, Christ was born of a woman. He performed His first miracle at the behest of a woman. It was a woman whom Jesus healed in the crowd when she reached out and touched His garment. It was women who first discovered that the tomb was empty. It was a woman He first appeared to after He rose from the dead.

Jesus commanded men to respect and love their wives so deeply that they would not even look at a woman lustfully, much less sleep with another woman. In Ephesians 5, the infamous chapter in which women are instructed to "submit" to their husbands, men are not let off the hook. Paul calls on women to show love and respect. But men he calls to die:

> Husbands, love your wives, just as Christ loved the church and gave himself up for her to make her holy, cleansing her by the washing with water through the word, and to present her to himself as a radiant church, without stain or wrinkle or any other blemish, but holy and blameless. In this same way, husbands ought to love their wives as their own bodies. He who loves his wife loves himself. After all, no one ever hated their own body, but they feed and care for their body, just as Christ does the church—for we are members of his body. "For this reason a man will leave his father and mother and be united to his wife, and the two will become one flesh." This is a profound mystery—but I am talking about Christ and the church. However, each one of you also must love his wife as he loves himself, and the wife must respect her husband.

Christianity liberated women the same as it liberated men. And it granted dignity to women the same as it granted dignity to men. All societies may not have put these commands into practice perfectly, but that does not change the fact that the commands were given. We never needed feminism. We already had the Gospels. After all, feminism merely wants to make women people. Christianity wants to make them saints. Along the same lines, a woman recently told me she's a feminist because she thinks a female should be able to walk to her car without worrying about getting mugged (I guess men should have to worry about it, or maybe she thinks we never do). I've heard this line, or lines like it, countless times and it never gets less disturbing. How is it that these people need "feminism" to tell them that women shouldn't be robbed in a parking lot? And how is it that they are so ignorant of world history that they think no other ideology or school of thought ever came up with the idea that women shouldn't be robbed, raped, and brutalized?

It's simply not true that women were oppressed for the entirety of human civilization until the emergence of the feminist movement. Feminists are often given credit for pioneering the idea that women should be able to do more than cook and clean and so on, but there was never a universal consensus that cooking and cleaning were all women should do in the first place.

LIBERATION BY INDUSTRIALIZATION

Often, we tie female liberation to the Industrial Age, equating the liberty of womanhood with women's ability and opportunity to work a job and participate in the American democratic system. Lost in this theory is the fact that Christian civilization—before the United States, before industrialization, possibly even before Gloria Steinem—afforded many rights to women. How often do you hear anyone mention that females were members in equal standing to men in the vast majority of the English guilds in the Middle Ages?

Yes, thanks to Christianity, there were women in many occupations and practicing many trades, long before we were all seduced by the siren song of the assembly line. The Industrial Age is much more responsible for dehumanizing people than humanizing them. It's another mark of the confusion of our era that we think women weren't truly "human" until they had their very own time card to punch.

In agrarian societies before industrialization, men and women, parents and children, all worked together in their fields and in their homes. It was not a glamorous life, but it was a life in which each member of the family had something to do, and knew that what he or she was doing was important and necessary. Everyone worked. Everyone contributed. Everyone did his or her part. These days, we're so averse to "roles," so opposed to letting our sex and our biology play any part in deciding what we do with ourselves, that we all ended up paralyzed. We don't play the role society tells us to play, nor do we play any other role at all.

It wasn't until men were removed from the home for work, and children for school, that women began to feel understandably marginalized and forgotten. Feminism's answer was to send women from the home as well, where they could supposedly rediscover their worth and dignity as numbers on someone's payroll sheet. Now nobody is at home, and that happiness and serenity humanity chased when it left the home still eludes us.

Maybe this is all academic, but it's necessary to establish that feminism wasn't a modern solution to an ancient problem—it was a modern solution to a modern problem. And a very flawed solution because it managed to perpetuate the very issues it set out to address.

THE MODERN VARIETY

It's clear that feminism was, from the start, a doomed vessel, even for its good ideas, because it politicized gender, preached an ideology of division and competition, and convinced women to seek their worth and dignity outside of the home. It would have been better to advocate that Christian principles be applied more completely and perfectly—much as the abolitionists did—rather than devising an ideology to compete with Christianity. The abolitionists may have spoken of "abolitionism," but it wasn't an ideology that lived past the death of slavery, as feminism has lived long past the battle for suffrage.

But now I think we should skip ahead and deal with what feminism is today. Because where feminism of old was a flawed ideology struggling to bring about some good and worthwhile changes, the feminism of our modern age is just a flawed ideology. The fight for women's rights is over in this country, so now feminists have embarked on a campaign to invent and claim new rights, which they call "women's rights."

"Women's rights" is, for certain, a meaningless phrase in modern American society, used by feminists to reinforce a fantasy of patriarchal oppression and systematic man-on-woman victimization. The Left relies heavily, almost exclusively, on false narratives, and the contemporary "fight for women's rights" is perhaps the greatest and falsest of all (although the competition for that title is quite stiff).

The Left talks about "women's rights" as a thing yet to be fully achieved; women in America are "second-class citizens," they breathlessly insist. Therefore, they say, the struggle for "women's rights" is not only a political issue but one of the biggest political issues we face, which is a bit like saying that smallpox is one of the biggest health issues we face.

It's worth noting that women aren't the only ones locked in an imaginary battle to secure legal protections they already have. The same could be said of gays and racial minorities and, to a certain extent, anyone who isn't a straight, white, Christian male.

These days, everyone has their own brand of rights (except for the unborn), and those rights are always under siege by some villainous phantom force, usually composed of Republicans, talk-radio hosts, and white men who vote for Republicans and listen to talk radio. Liberals conjure up trendy new categories of rights about once a week, with recent additions like "transgender rights," "obese rights," "vegan rights," "air traveler rights," and "demisexual genderqueer transspecies Wiccan rights." Everyone's engaged in a campaign for mythological rights in modern America—again, with the exception of the ones who can be legally decapitated and sold for parts. They don't count, remember.

But of all these categories, none result in more screaming, screeching, complaining, and hashtagging than "women's rights" (well, second only to "gay rights"). This is particularly ironic, considering women—the born ones, anyway—not only fare perfectly well in our society but in many cases do quite a bit better than anyone else. While feminists prattle on about their alleged inequality in America, women continue to benefit from profound legal privileges like affirmative action and Title IX, and routinely receive lighter sentences than men—for the same crimes—in federal court.

FORGOTTEN MEN

Feminism takes issues that afflict all human beings—struggles and tribulations that are inherent to life on Earth for all people—and twists them into a fantastical drama of man versus woman. And when feminists concentrate solely and exclusively on the real and imagined plight of women, the obvious insinuation is that men have it easier. This, again, is why gender should not be made into its own ideology. There's nothing wrong with striving to help women get a leg up, but being a feminist almost always means ignoring, for instance, the fact that boys face a school system that is 70 percent more likely to suspend them and a medical establishment that's twice as likely to diagnose them with learning disabilities.

They can call a man's challenges less severe, but they never explain why guys kill themselves at a rate four times higher, and face a much higher probability of developing substance-abuse disorders. And they talk about violence against women but they don't mention that men are 76 percent more likely to be the victims of murder. These are not all matters of "rights," obviously, but they prove that our society is not lavishing advantages on men.

As far as rights go, women have more than almost anyone else. Notably, women are the sole authorities empowered to be judge, jury, and executioner of children. That's certainly not an entitlement I envy or desire, but it is an unprecedented legal power not granted to men.

At no point in America's allegedly sexist past have things gotten so sexist that any man could go around murdering babies without facing legal repercussions.

Note that I'm talking here about Western society in North America and Europe. I'm aware that women in other parts of the world—Muslim countries, mostly— are still very often deprived of dignity and liberty. But, because I'm sort of a stickler for logic, I have to point out that even Saudi Arabia doesn't have a "women's rights" issue, per se. It has a human rights issue. It's reductive to look at the transgressions of Arab dictators or terrorist groups and accuse them of infringing simply on "women's rights." They dehumanize women, clearly, but the problem stretches far beyond that.

Wherever women are subjugated in the Middle East, so too are Christians of both sexes, Muslims of the wrong variety, people of lower social classes, and basically any other group that isn't favored by those in power. I daresay ISIS treats Muslim women (of the right branch) comparatively better than they treat Christian men. And I say that because any treatment is better than being marched out into the desert and shot to death.

So we could break it down and categorize each type of right desecrated by Muslim barbarians—non-Muslim women's rights, Christian rights, gay rights, ethnic minority rights, etc.—or we could just say that ISIS has a problem with human rights, period. They may infringe on these rights differently depending on who you are (women are raped, men are cooked alive), but the only ones granted "rights" at all are those who fit into the narrow category prescribed by whoever happens to be holding the gun at any particular moment.

In any case, when the Left talks about fighting for women's rights, they usually aren't referring to the Middle East anyway. Even though I think the very term *women's rights* is philosophically problematic, I would have no qualms at all if feminists went to Muslim lands to concentrate all their efforts there. In fact, if any feminist gender-studies professor or *Cosmopolitan* editor wants to travel to Iran to continue her mission of female liberation, I will happily pay for the plane ticket. But they do no such thing, which makes the "feminist movement" all the more pointless and intellectually dishonest.

Politicians tout their devotion to "women's rights" on their campaign websites, but rarely do they make any specific mention of the women being sexually brutalized and murdered by Islamists overseas. Instead, they vow to fight for women's "equal rights" and "equal opportunity" here in America, despite the rather relevant detail that women already have equal rights and equal opportunity here in America. These politicians might as well start organizing rallies to repeal nationwide alcohol prohibition and the Fugitive Slave Act while they're at it.

IMAGINARY PERSECUTIONS

Of course, liberals will claim that women are still deprived of rights because of the "wage gap" and "rape culture" and alleged conservative assaults on "reproductive health," but even if these were legitimate issues, they wouldn't have anything at all to do with equal rights. Yes, women are victims of violence in this country, but none of the violence is legal. When a woman is raped, her legal rights have not been violated by the State but by a person. So even if there were a veritable "rape epidemic" in our society, it wouldn't be at all an issue of women possessing unequal legal rights or protections.

As it happens, though, while rape is obviously a real and terrible phenomenon, the so-called American "rape epidemic" is a dangerous fable concocted by the Left. In fact, rape is another area in which women possess more legal rights than men. Many colleges have rape tribunals set up that allow women to make anonymous rape accusations against men, who will then face severe penalties even if no evidence was ever presented against them. Worse still, if two drunk people have sex on a college campus, the man can be accused of rape the next day on the basis that a consenting drunk person cannot give consent.

By that logic, women should frequently find themselves expelled or in prison for drunk hookups as well, but that never happens. Men are the only ones who can be accused of rape simply because the woman regrets what she did the next day. If "rape culture" creates unequal legal protections for anyone, it's men.

Likewise, the "wage gap" is a faulty basis from which to prove that women still lack equal rights in this country. This "gap" is not something instituted by the government, or by anyone, actually, because it's a work of fiction. Not only does the wage gap not exist, but there's already been a law passed to alleviate the nonexistent problem. It's a fake problem that's been fake-solved by bad laws and dumb regulations.

Do women make "seventy-seven cents for every dollar men earn"? Sure, according to some figures. But that statistic is about as meaningful as saying, "Women give birth to one hundred percent of the babies" or "Women spend a billion dollars more each year at the gynecologist." All of these things are probably true, but to cite them in an effort to prove discrimination is ridiculous.

The "seventy-seven cents" figure lies by omission. Purposefully left out of the equation are relevant details like: tenure, job title, hours worked, region, experience, skill level, industry, occupation, safety risks, education level, and difficulty. The figure simply compares all women and all men who work—however poorly or however competently—for over thirty-five hours in any job, in any part of the country, for any period of time, at any experience level.

A receptionist working thirty-eight hours a week at your local dentist's office is evenly stacked up against a stockbroker or a coal miner. The salary of a male neurosurgeon is compared to that of a female manicurist. A male electrician is contrasted with a Denny's waitress.

In all cases, the disparity is shoved under the "wage gap" blanket, and used to paint a picture of sexism and paternalistic oppression.

The reality is this: Men are more likely to work dangerous, physically demanding, high-stress jobs. They're more likely to work weekends and holidays. They're more likely to be willing to relocate. They're more likely to pursue jobs in higher-paying fields.

Loggers and steelworkers are paid well, but the job requires the sort of brute force that most women don't possess. A job on an offshore oil rig will pay handsomely because of the risks, the physical nature of the work, and the demands it places on your time. You will find more men taking these positions than women, but are we ready to chalk that up to "discrimination"? Will the average feminist college grad actually travel to North Dakota to find a job drilling for oil, thereby helping to alleviate the nefarious wage gap, or will she stay at home and look for something easier to do, but then spend her spare time complaining that no women are out there drilling for oil in North Dakota?

Women business owners earn 50 percent less than

men business owners. Does this mean that women business owners are discriminating against themselves? Does it mean that the State is conspiring to stop women from opening businesses? The State does make it enormously difficult for anyone to become an entrepreneur, but does anyone actually believe—and can they provide evidence to prove—that the government makes it even more cumbersome for women?

Probably not.

So seventy-seven cents on the dollar? OK, and . . . ? What does that prove?

This is the kind of math done only by politicians and propagandists. If you need workable and realistic numbers—statistics that tell you something important or relevant or even slightly functional—you would, obviously, control for factors that threaten to wildly skew your data, that disproportionately impact the equation, and that fog your ultimate conclusion.

Yet, because the "women's rights" narrative must be supported, we still hear about this crisis that a three-minute Google search will reveal as bogus. Liberals are never satisfied, even when they get exactly what they want to address an issue they fabricated out of thin air.

The Left's crusade for "women's rights" is an obnoxious, insidious farce, a lie designed to drive a wedge between the sexes and sow seeds of division and suspicion. Liberal feminists will say they don't hate men, but in truth, their "women's rights" narrative is fueled only by hatred. They envy men, resent children, and detest themselves.

A feminist will say that women are not "equal" in America, and she'll try to prove her point by making up these various systematic anti-woman tyrannies, but really, when it comes down to it, she means that women are not equal to men simply because they are not men. That's her real beef. She does not want women to have equal protection under the law—as we've seen, she wants, and has, greater protection. What she really desires is sameness.

The feminist loathes her own nature. She wants to be as men are, and wants men to stop being as they are and become as she is. Feminism presents masculinity as the ideal while also tearing it down. It hates men because they're men, and women because they aren't. It is, in short, an insane and delusional philosophy. But because it cannot be brought to actual fruition, the feminist demands we all cooperate with—and submit to—the delusion.

REAL PERSECUTIONS

With all of this said, there are a few areas where, admittedly, our culture particularly degrades women. These are not "women's rights" issues, but human issues that seem to especially impact the fairer sex. First is the evil, repugnant pornography industry that primarily trades in the debasement and objectification of women and children. And we've already talked about the other two areas where women are degraded and demeaned: transgenderism and abortion.

Pornography, transgenderism, abortion. These are the real enemies of women in our culture. They defile everything that makes a woman unique, beautiful, and true. But you'll notice that feminists, with rare exception, are not referring to these areas when they talk about "women's rights." On the contrary, they claim that these are avenues of female empowerment.

The feminist discussion of "women's rights" is not meant to help women. At best, it's intended only to justify the continued existence of feminism, and at worst, it denigrates men, oppresses children, and provides cover to those who harm women.

Women have equal rights and then some in this country, but they still face their own struggles. Those struggles need to be met head-on, but feminism isn't up to the task. It's too busy fighting battles it already won last century and claiming sole ownership of ideas that existed hundreds of years before its proponents started lecturing about "male privilege" at our universities.

If you believe that women should not be systematically oppressed by the government—good. I agree with you. Almost everybody agrees with you. That belief just makes you a constitutionalist.

If you believe that women possess an inherent worth and dignity equal to that of men—great. I agree with you. That belief makes you Christian, or at least brings you closer to becoming one.

All of the ground is covered; there is no need for feminism. Whatever good could have been found is now covered in piles of death and hatred, and no matter what anyone wants to believe, the roots of "bad feminism" can be traced back to "good feminism." It's all connected. Saying that you need to cling to feminism just because you believe in equal protection under the law is like saying that you have to join an anarchist cell just to be a proponent of smaller government.

So there is no need for feminism, unless you wish to tinker with the definitions of "equal protection" and "inherent worth and dignity," so as to justify things like abortion-on-demand and taxpayer-subsidized birth control.

For that, you do need feminism, and that's why society would be better off without it.

10

The Inequality of the Sexes

WHY MEETING IN THE MIDDLE
MAKES FOR A MUDDLE

With all due respect to Thomas Jefferson, we are not created equal. Equality means sameness, and sameness is achieved when two things are absolutely identical, devoid of any unique or distinctive features. Sameness is a mathematical reality, not a sociological one. Even in mathematics, two only equals two on paper, in the abstract.

In reality, two apples don't really equal two apples, and two elephants don't really equal two elephants, because the elephants and the apples are all different shapes and sizes and densities and so on. If you have two apples and I have two apples, one of us has more apple than the other. Parents learn this the hard way, especially parents of twins, because when you give both kids an apple, or a lollipop, or a handful of Goldfish, or whatever, they'll promptly compare their hauls, and the one who ended up with less, even though you gave them equal amounts, will demand restitution.

So nothing is equal. That's the lesson I teach my daughter when she complains that her brother got the bigger apple, and that's the lesson society needs to learn for itself. Nothing is equal and nobody is equal.

In the abstract—spiritually, in this case—you can say that we are all equal in human worth and dignity, but even here caveats are necessary. It is true that all human beings have dignity and worth that should not be diminished or ignored. And it is true that our dignity and worth are not tied to our development, physical capabilities, or participation in the consumer economy. Our souls transcend this physical plane, and one day most of the things that we think set us apart will melt away in the face of our Almighty God.

But I don't anticipate, when that point arrives, that I'll be judged as dignified and worthy as Mother Teresa or Saint Paul or Moses, and should I make it to Heaven—a hierarchical place, we should note—I don't expect to receive quite the same due (2 Corinthians 5:10) as those great and humble servants of the Lord. If I am entirely "equal" in dignity and worth to Saint Peter or Saint Augustine, if I am equal in any way at all, I can't see how that will ever manifest itself, or what the point is in say-ing it. It's clear that all human beings are human beings, but even at the transcendent level, that appears to be where our similarities end.

The only other area where equality even theoreti-cally exists is in matters of law. It's considered a sacred American principle that all people should be equal under the law, and of course this idea was officially codified in 1866, with the Equal Protection Clause of the Four-teenth Amendment:

> All persons born or naturalized in the United States, and subject to the jurisdiction thereof, are citizens of the United States and of the State wherein they reside. No State shall make or en-force any law which shall abridge the privileges or immunities of citizens of the United States; nor shall any State deprive any person of life, liberty, or property, without due process of law; nor deny to any person within its jurisdiction the equal pro-tection of the laws.

It would seem a heresy to argue against the rather nice-sounding notion that all people should be guaran-teed equal protection under the law, but I don't need to argue against it because it's not real. Unborn children are not protected by the law at all, much less equally. The tax code treats people differently based on their income and a dozen other things. Obamacare grants deals, loopholes, entitlements, and levies, and it mandates penalties and pardons, based on age, economic status, and a host of other factors. Felons are not allowed to vote or buy handguns, which is a law that doesn't apply to anyone else. Sex offenders have to register in a database, which is a requirement not currently imposed on anyone else. Kids have to sit at home dejected and bored while everyone else plays the lottery and drinks hard liquor, both being privileges unequally and discriminatorily granted.

I'm not against all of these inequalities, but the relevant fact is that they are inequalities, and I could have listed countless other examples. "Equal protection under the law," if taken literally, would mean we are all affected by every law in exactly the same way, to exactly the same extent, with exactly the same personal and financial consequences. But that is not how it works, and indeed it could never work that way. The law should not pretend it can't distinguish at all between one sort of person or the other. That would be madness. It might be equal if the law saw no distinction between you and a serial rapist, but would it be just?

As it stands, the Equal Protection Clause has become an outlet for Supreme Court justices to randomly convert their ideologies into constitutional law. Thus, the court found that the Fourteenth Amendment protects a woman's right to kill her child, and more recently, that it guaranteed a homosexual's right to get "married." Oddly, it still does not protect a child's right to continue living. This is what we call "equal" in our culture, further proving my point that equality is not a thing that can be found in reality, nor something we should actually strive to achieve. It would be more accurate to say that all people should be treated as people, but not necessarily as the same people.

Beyond the legal and the spiritual, equality most certainly does not exist in any physical sense. Some of us are smarter than others, some of us stronger, some of us wiser, more honest, more disciplined, more talented, more virtuous. You might be a better person than me by just about every measure. Or maybe I'm a better person than you. But what is certain is that you are not the same person as me, and we are not, by any discernible standard, equal. If I compare Stephen Hawking to Steph Curry, I will struggle to find a single area of equality or commonality between them.

It reveals the egotism rampant in our culture that we so breathlessly insist on our "equality" with everyone else. You'll notice that these claims of equality are almost always wielded as a means to drag another person down, rarely to lift anyone up. You don't often hear a passerby declare that he is equal to the bum sitting on the curb drinking a 25-ounce can of Natural Ice in the middle of the day. More likely, he'll save those declarations for his neighbor with a better job, a happier marriage, and better-behaved kids.

This arrogance is what has led to the leveling of society, where the distinctions between class and status and accomplishment have eroded, with everyone consolidating in the center. These days, our poor have all of the vices of the wealthy—greed, materialism, superficiality—and the wealthy have the vices of the poor—crudeness, vulgarity, classlessness. We've all met here in the middle, in the name of an equality that has mainly been achieved by adopting all of the worst traits of our neighbors.

This is what the struggle for equality has done. It doesn't make people better. It makes them afraid to be better, and it makes others jealous of those who are better. If we structured our culture around, rather than the pursuit of equality, the pursuit and advancement of virtue, we would end up with a society organized into classes, but it would be a better society. Or at least it would be a society ordered toward making people better, instead of merely making them the same.

We say we are equal because we don't want anyone to be treated better or to be seen as better than us. We aren't quite as concerned about the folks who are treated worse and seen as worse. But, as difficult as this may be to confront, the people in the former camp may actually be better than us. The world is full of war heroes and rocket scientists and abusive deadbeats and soup kitchen volunteers and greedy hoarders and philanthropists and surgeons and saints and villains and martyrs and all sorts of people in between. What it is not filled with—what you cannot find anywhere outside of a math textbook—is equality. And if equality cannot be found between individuals, it surely cannot be found between the sexes.

THE GENDER EQUALITY MYTH

As I've taken great pains to establish, one man cannot be called equal to another man, and one woman cannot be called equal to another woman. And if there is no real, substantive, actionable, observable equality within the ranks of each gender, how could we possibly claim that any sort of equality could ever be achieved *between* them? I am not equal to John, but at least we have in common that we are men. I am not equal to Jane, and we don't even have that in common.

Men and women are not equal. They can never be equal. It has not happened. It will not happen. It cannot happen. My wife is not and will not be equal to me, and I will not be equal to her. I am a man, she is a woman, and that is only where our vast but complementary (usually) differences begin. If my wife were equal to me, if she were the same as me, I would not have married her. I am already me, after all. What first attracted me to her is precisely that she is very emphatically not me. The last thing I want is to be married to myself. Why my wife desired such a fate is a question I will spend my whole life pondering.

"Gender equality" is a figment of the progressive imagination. It has no bearing in the real world. And the efforts to bring this Orwellian fantasy to life, efforts under way by both transgenders and feminists (I suppose this common but preposterous goal explains why the two have not yet set out to destroy each other), can only result in further confusion and division, ironically creating more of the inequality these groups hope to cure.

Our culture hopes to establish "gender equality" in three areas: legal, social, and physical. We've already discussed the freakish and horrifying campaign to render the physical distinctions between the sexes irrelevant. As for legal equality, we've seen that the law does not treat men and women the same, and the people who claim to be fighting for such a result are mostly fighting to ensure that women are, like the privileged pigs in *Animal Farm*, treated "more equally."

Legal equality between the sexes is a myth. It has not been accomplished, it won't be, and it shouldn't be. In order for the law to treat the sexes the same, it would have to pretend that the sexes are the same. This makes about as much sense as drafting a tax code that treats the numbers seven and sixteen as the same, or buying a cookbook that treats T-bone steak and chicken breasts as the same. That's not to say men should be treated better than women, or vice versa, but that men should always be treated as men because they are men, and women as women because they are women.

I'm not advocating for a return to the Victorian era (although in many instances, it would be an improvement over the current one). I'm simply noting that total and absolute equality under the law—a law that never makes any distinction between men and women—is an absurdity. And the more we try to attain it, the more we end up with laws that put cross-dressing men in the women's restroom and women on the frontlines of the battlefield.

SOCIAL EQUALITY

Full legal equality will never happen, and physical equality is impossible, but social equality can be effectively achieved, God help us, so long as we continue our collective march into moral and intellectual oblivion. That march doesn't appear to be slowing down, so the Left's androgynous paradise may soon be brought to fruition.

We will have so-called social equality when the last vestiges of "traditional gender roles" are annihilated and our society finally treats men and women as totally indistinguishable. A society that desires a social gender equality is a society that resists anything and everything that is uniquely masculine or feminine.

This crusade is often physically violent. So violent, in fact, that when all is said and done, "gender equality" will have killed more people and destroyed more lives than all the wars and tyrants in history. That is probably already the case, when you consider the fifty million children aborted in the world each year. Most of them were slaughtered so that women might be liberated from their own biology and made as barren as men. Millions of children have been cut to pieces and thrown into the trash so that their mothers could spurn motherhood, thereby attaining that fabled equality.

This consuming desire for equality with men has made many feminist women actively hostile even to the idea of children. Feminists lash out angrily at women who extol the virtues of motherhood, as evidenced by the outrage that erupted a little while ago when the pop singer Adele confessed that being a mother gave her "purpose." Many liberal women were upset at this proclamation, because motherhood is apparently far too feminine for a feminist. To them, motherhood is a very particular and different and unique sort of thing. It is not an expression of "gender equality" but a profound and glorious repudiation of it.

Perhaps this is why President Obama once famously worried aloud that his daughters might one day be "punished with a baby." Echoing Obama's sentiments, last year *Cosmopolitan* printed an article lamenting the fact that the birth rate in Texas rose slightly after stiffer abortion regulations were passed in the state. The magazine tweeted a link to its article with the text "Texas women are having more babies since Planned Parenthood was defunded," accompanied by a sad-face emoji. In the feminist view, childbirth is an occasion for sad faces. That's why feminists are a total bummer to have around at baby showers.

If progressive feminists had their way, no woman would ever become a mother again. There would simply be no more children, until—and if—we reach a point where babies can be conceived, grown, and cultivated in petri dishes, and then purchased by a husband and wife, or a single woman, or a pair of lesbians, or a trio of homosexual men, or a man and his octopus bride.

The whole process of conception, pregnancy, and birth is far too specific and exclusive. Far too womanly. Far too unequal. That's why it must be rejected, and why babies must become collateral damage in the war for equality.

GENDER NORMS

Our culture has convinced itself that "conformity" and "norms" are universally bad things. And in this realm of

bad things, we believe that nothing is worse than conformity to gender norms. The propagators of these dreaded
gender norms (including, as we discovered, transgenders)
pin the label "feminine" on women and the label "masculine" on men, and then ruthlessly restrict each group
to its respective area. At least that's how they teach it at
college.

The push against gender norms must necessarily start
in the cradle, where parents are encouraged to let children express themselves in whatever way they desire, offering no guidance at all, especially not guidance that
directs boys toward boyish things and girls toward girl-
ish things. Children, we're told, can be whatever they
want to be.

So if your eight-year-old boy wants to adorn himself
in blouses and fingernail polish, he (or she or xe or whatever pronoun the prepubescent child chooses for himself
or herself or xyrself) should not be prevented from doing
so. If your teenage son wants to dress like Mary Poppins
and flutter off to school, he should not be steered away
from this behavior.

The very idea of offering a child direction and guidance is offensive to many liberals. Recently, I gave a talk
on gender at a particularly liberal university in Califor-
nia (I'm not sure they have any other kind of university
over there). During the Q&A, a student demanded to
know what I would do if my son decided he'd like to wear

a skirt one day. I said I'd instruct my son not to wear the skirt, and explain why. The student was incredulous.

"You mean you'd tell him no? Can you imagine how that would make him *feel*?"

I can somewhat excuse the student's naïveté, considering he has no children of his own, has very little experience dealing with children, and apparently is suffering from amnesia about his own childhood. But any competent parent understands that little kids have to be told no all the time. Every day. Every hour. Sometimes every minute.

Kids are always looking for ways to unintentionally maim or kill themselves. As soon as my son comes barreling into a room, the first thing he thinks is, *What's the most dangerous and reckless thing I can possibly do here?* And both he and his sister always find it. Once, not long ago, I left the kids in the living room by themselves for ninety seconds so I could use the bathroom, and when I came back, my son was dancing on top of the radiator and my daughter was running around with the pointy end of a pencil in her mouth.

It's in these moments that I think my children might actually be insane. But then I remember that they're children, and that children are insane by nature. They understand very little about the world, and they are hardly concerned at all with ordering their actions by what is safe, hygienic, normal, and reasonable. That's where my wife and I enter the picture. That's why we have to be there, literally every second of the day, constantly shepherding them along the right and healthy path.

So that means telling kids no. A lot. And it means teaching them and showing them the sort of things they are supposed to do and the sort of people they are supposed to be. If my wife and I are not willing to do that, then we should have adopted a pair of gerbils instead of conceiving a set of tiny human beings. Kids need guidance and instruction, and that includes guidance and instruction about how to properly express and live out their genders.

Yes, girls can sometimes have masculine traits and do masculine things and boys feminine, but the girl should still be taught what it means to be a girl and the boy what it means to be a boy. Gender norms and gender roles exist to help men and women fit into society in ways that are best suited for them.

We attack the gender norms merely because they're norms, but nobody ever explains what's actually wrong with them. Yes, when you're dealing with such a broad subject, you can always find examples that truly are, as the feminists might say, problematic. But our culture has waged an assault on norms universally, and attempted to throw them all down the garbage disposal as punishment for existing in the first place.

Yet, as liberalism conjures up its various gender theories, I still see, like so many billions of parents before me, a natural inclination in my own son and daughter to seek what is masculine and what is feminine, respectively. And I see masculine and feminine traits, manifested by a budding protectiveness and strength in my son and a gentleness and nurturing in my daughter. I'm told so often that boys and girls yearn for ambiguity, but here are my children, just three years old, already reinforcing gender norms like a couple of right-wing extremists. They need guidance in discovering and becoming themselves, but that guidance should be directed toward fostering this innate recognition that children already possess.

Nobody ever said that girls can't be strong or that boys can't be gentle, but there is something automatic, particular, unique, and complementary about the boy's strength and the girl's gentleness. And that is good. It's who they are. It's who God intended them to be. Liberal parents claim they want to avoid imposing gender norms on their children, but often they end up imposing the opposite of the gender norm. They create a new norm, which is defined only in the negative. The empowered modern woman is empowered not because she's powerful but because she acts like she's not a woman. The enlightened man is enlightened not because he's enlightened but because he's not masculine.

Our culture doesn't have any new ideas about genders, just prejudices against the old ideas. All you have to do to prove the point is skim through Google and find feminist mommy bloggers lamenting the fact that their daughters, despite the best efforts of these mothers, still like to wear pink and dress up in tutus. What sort of selfish and arrogant parent goes out of her way to specifically avoid letting her daughter play with "girly" things? These are kids, not experiments in a sociology class. To steer your daughter intentionally away from femininity is not parenting; it's activism.

Disturbingly, there are many activists out there raising kids, and not enough parents.

Femininity, it might be said, is womanhood's gift to the world, and masculinity is manhood's gift. We need men to be masculine and women to be feminine so that women can also have masculine traits and men feminine. If you want to adopt some parts of the Italian culture, the process will be made more difficult if Italy doesn't have an Italian culture. It's just like how the pro-immigration types think America should open its doors to everyone, yet they forget that nobody can benefit from being American if America is not American itself. Now I'm getting sidetracked, but you get the point. Women can't be masculine if men are not masculine, because then there is no masculinity.

This is why it's advisable for a child to have both a mom and dad around (revolutionary concept these days, I realize), so they can learn about femininity and masculinity, and gradually grow into a personality that's influenced by both. A girl's identity will be fortified by the example of her mother, who demonstrates womanly traits, and the example of her father, who demonstrates the masculine. Importantly, she'll also learn how the two should treat and love each other, and what that looks like in practice.

This lesson will be essential later, when she starts to date. If she has a good father, she can look at her boyfriend and ask herself, *Would my father treat my mother this way?* If the answer is no, she'll realize the boy is a jerk, and she'll drop the loser and move on. On the flip side, if she has a bad or absent father, she'll ask the same question of the same jerk, come to the conclusion that the answer is yes, and continue dating him.

Gender is not arbitrary or unimportant. Without a proper understanding of it, our children will be confused not only about who they are but about how they should treat, and be treated by, the opposite sex. There is a certain biological and spiritual imperative that comes with our sex. When we teach our kids to reject it, we doom them to a life of failed relationships and internal turmoil.

The social equality movement makes members of both sexes less grateful for the other by convincing each that they can easily fill both roles. It breeds contention in the place of appreciation. It tells a young girl that she can do whatever boys can do, which causes her to see boys as competition—obstacles to be leaped over and knocked to the side on her journey toward success and self-discovery.

As both genders run from themselves, hiding from anything that reminds them of who they ought to be, we finally converge somewhere in the dull, strange middle, where men dress like manicured prepubescent boys who accidentally fell into a vat of women's clothes on clearance at the thrift store. Surprisingly, we come to understand that the line of distinction between genders is exactly what allows the members of both to express themselves in different and unique ways. Blur the lines, and we all end up faded and dull.

11

The Darkest Night

HOW TO WIN A WAR
WHEN IT'S ALREADY OVER

As I've established over the past many pages, liberalism is itself defined by its rejection of objective truth. The opposition movement, it stands to reason, should be primarily defined by its defense of that truth. But what is objective truth?

Well, we know what it is not. Objective truth is not the truth imagined or concocted by any individual person, or group of people, for their own advantage or convenience. It is not the truth arbitrarily decreed by some government edict or presidential directive. It is not the truth dictated by the fashions of the moment or embraced by the popular culture or demanded by this or that mob.

No.

The truth we accept and protect and give voice to is timeless. It is eternal. It comes from the God who created the universe and everything in it.

It has been revealed to the human race over centuries and millennia by God's prophets and most especially by His Son, Jesus Christ. It has been illuminated and explained by history's greatest thinkers and philosophers, from Aristotle to Aquinas to Burke to Lewis.

This truth is, we should constantly remind the world, accessible by human reason. It is innate. It is ingrained in all of us from birth. This is why we find ourselves constantly battling ideas nobody actually believes, such as the idea that men can be women if they put on a dress. It is objectively untrue, and contrary to reason; thus, everyone who is not mentally ill already, at some level, knows it.

And that truth, objective truth, revolves around and hinges on the answer to one question, which according to Christian tradition was first asked at the dawn of time by the Archangel Michael, when he issued his immortal challenge to the fallen angel Lucifer: Who is like God?

This question has rung down through the ages. It seems, in fact, that every generation of human beings is called upon to answer it.

And the leaders of nations who've given a false and evil answer, who've claimed, as in the case of the totalitarian nightmares of the twentieth century, that the government is like God and that the government is the source of "truth"—these leaders have led their nations to catastrophe and the world to orgies of bloodshed and ruin.

Which brings us to our own generation and nation.

OUR ONLY MISSION

The United States of America was founded on the proposition that human rights and dignity come from God, that every human being is entitled to life, liberty, and the pursuit of happiness by virtue of being a creature of God. Our Declaration of Independence states this explicitly, and our Constitution flows from that premise.

Yet now in this modern age of the twenty-first century, a new power has arisen, and that power and those who champion it presume to overturn the wisdom of the ages and the foundational principles of our democracy.

To do this, they answer the ancient question of the Archangel Michael with the oldest lie of human history: That we—or they, anyway—are like God. That the "truth" is only what we—they—say it is. That the moral code is relative and malleable, subject to human preferences and whims.

And there are no better and easier vehicles with which to foist this ancient fraud on the nation than the three foundational issues of life, sex, and gender. These issues go directly and viscerally to our humanity, to who we are and who we strive to be. Our understanding of these issues must be rooted in this eternal and objective truth, or we will very quickly lose our bearings, and eventually our humanity.

Conservatism is a movement that defends truth. Moral truths, scientific truths, spiritual truths, legal truths. Conservatism does not own these truths—it did not invent them—but every era requires some force to rise up and defend them, to "conserve" them, and so here we are.

You only ever hear about conservation as it pertains to the environment these days. And, for the record, I'm not opposed to "conserving" the beauty of the natural world. Indeed, I've never met anyone fundamentally opposed to nature or the environment, despite the fact that liberals often tag conservatives as "anti-environment," which would make about as much sense as being anti-gravity or anti-elephants. The environment is a physical reality. I am not one to deny physical realities. That's what liberals do.

In any case, there is more to conserve than trees and three-toed sloths. Conservatives seek—or should seek—to conserve the experience and wisdom of millennia of human existence, and the laws passed down by the fathers of our nation and codified into our founding documents. Liberals see these truths and teachings and laws as chains that must be broken. They reject most of what was given to us by the past because it all reeks of Christianity. And sometimes they reject it for no other reason than its date of origin.

However the names *conservative* and *liberal* originally came to be and whatever they used to mean, this is what they mean today. Liberals seek liberation from the laws and truths that have governed mankind for centuries, while conservatives, what few exist, believe that our ancestors did not live and fight and die for those truths for nothing, and that they should not be tossed aside just because they fail to jibe with the trends of our era.

This is the only mission of conservatism, or whatever you want to call it: the truth. The truth is the end, the final good, the only good. The truth is our only chance, and nothing else will do.

We must prefer the truth over anything. We must take the truth over winning friends or respect or admiration or elections. We must take the truth over party, over country, over life itself. Henry David Thoreau said, "Rather than love, than money, than fame, give me truth."

That should be our attitude. An insatiable hunger for it, a pathological obsession with it, a militant protectiveness of it. This is what so endlessly frustrates me. We have the truth on our side, yet we sit around perplexed about how to reach people, how to motivate them. We have the truth on our side, but we continue to think it's not enough, or maybe it's too much. We have the truth on our side, but we don't use it as a sword to impale those who advance against it.

The truth is what wins a person's heart and mind. The truth is what lights a fire inside them. The truth motivates. The truth stirs the apathetic and wakes the sleeping. It moves the sedentary and excites the lethargic. The truth destroys tyrants and builds empires.

ANGER ROOTED IN PASSION FOR TRUTH

When did we stop caring about the truth? For God's sake, people have died for the truth. History is littered with the graves of heroes who've so believed in truth—the truth, not a truth, or their truth, or some truth, but *the* truth—that they gave up their very existence to protect it. That's what the truth does. And we have that on our side. We have the truth on our side: a weapon unmatched by any bomb or gun, a key that can unlock any door, a light that can illuminate any darkness. We have that, and often we're too afraid to stand by it, to use it, to speak it, to fight for it, to defend it against attacks from the outside and from within.

I've said a lot about the fear of conservatives and Christians who do not stand for their beliefs because they are paralyzed by the thought of being ostracized and rejected by society. But I think the greater problem is this lack of desire and passion, this detachment and disinterest. Fear lies at the bottom of that—to some extent, fear is at the bottom of all human weakness, at least according to Yoda.

I don't pretend to be the most fearless warrior for truth, or even a fearless warrior at all, but I am still grieved by the lack of passion and fire on the Right. There's plenty of anger, sure, but more of a bored, restless, dissatisfied anger. Not an anger rooted in a passion for truth.

Much of the fault for that, I believe, goes to the churches. Christians should be the fiercest soldiers for truth, but, in the West anyway, we've grown timid. The Christianity found in this country so often lacks edge and depth and passion. Walk into your average American church and you will not find very many signs that this is a faith with a sense of its own ancient and epic history. There is little sacredness to be found. Little pain, or beauty, or reverence.

Christianity has all of these things, fundamentally and totally, but many modern Christians in every denomination have spent many years trying to blunt them or bury them under a thousand layers of icing and whipped cream.

Everywhere you go, it seems, even in our houses of worship, there is this dullness, this sense that we're all just biding our time and waiting to get home so we can turn on the TV again.

I can't provide a remedy for that, exactly. We could try prayer. Maybe buckets of cold water over the head. I don't know. Our society seems to be constructed specifically to distract us from caring about important things. I am guilty of distraction and apathy. Thinking about the state of the world distresses me, and when I start mindlessly scrolling through Facebook or flipping through channels or searching desperately through my Netflix queue, the worries dissipate and I become numb. Sometimes I am tempted to stay in that numbness for as long as possible, because it's easier, it's more fun.

I think that's why we walk around with our heads buried in our phones. We'd rather look down because it's more comfortable than looking up and seeing the world and being forced to think about it, or do something about it. So I get it. But if we want to reclaim our culture, we have to look at it, and think about it, and care about it.

THRIVING IN OCCUPIED TERRITORY

I choose the word *reclaim* purposefully, because one can only reclaim something once it is lost. And our culture is lost. We hear quite often about the so-called "culture war," but there really is no war at present. We've been defeated, tragically. We failed. The culture is lost. I'm sorry. Whether some new assault may be mounted and a new war waged in the future is a different discussion. But as for the conflict referred to as the "culture war," the details are now a matter of history. We lost. Today we are a conquered people living in occupied territory. That will be our children's fate as well. I wish this weren't the case, but denying the reality will not change the facts of it.

I don't know the exact date of our defeat and surrender, but I can look over the landscape of American society and see very clearly that we were defeated and that we did surrender. The realities I have chronicled in this book are not signs of a battle for the culture. They are flags planted in the ground by a conquering army. In a culture war, the enemy tries to convince the population to accept and celebrate relativism, infanticide, perversion, and hedonism. Once it succeeds, the war is over. The enemy won. It did exactly what it wanted to do, and now it will set out to further humiliate and degrade the forces it just vanquished.

So we're the losers here. And we probably lost, or had all but lost, before I was born. Our parents (not mine, specifically) ushered in the sexual revolution, the divorce epidemic, fatherless homes, crack, AIDS, abortion, and so on when we were still in diapers. And because many of us were latchkey kids raised in empty houses and chaotic families, where cartoons and video games acted as baby-sitters, we are ill-equipped to win the battles from which our parents fled. It is a dire situation, I'm afraid.

That's the bad news. And there's a lot of it.

But there is some good news, and I think it was aptly illustrated in a very politically incorrect movie called *Zulu*, released in the 1960s.

"BECAUSE WE'RE HERE, LAD"

The film tells the story of one hundred and fifty British soldiers in South Africa who faced an onslaught of about four thousand Zulu warriors. In a scene toward the end, as the tired and injured soldiers await the attack, know-ing they will soon die, a young enlisted man turns to an older officer and asks, "Why does it have to be us? Why us?"

"Because we're here, lad," the officer responds. "And nobody else. Just us."

So it is for us. We're here, and nobody else. And we should be honored that God chose us to be here, under these conditions, at this point in history, in the middle of a desert, surrounded by the enemy. Fighting against odds that seem hopeless, and may very well be. At least in the short term.

There is really no reason to believe that we, or our children, can reverse decades of spiritual decay and moral rot. It feels like the end of Western civilization as we know it, and maybe it is. Decades from now, our grandchildren might be living in neighborhoods where the last church was demolished long ago. If we continue along this trajectory, it is hard to fathom the consequences. And I simply don't know that we have the power to reverse the course.

But it's not our lot to be fortune-tellers peering into a crystal ball. And it may not be our lot to "save America," whatever that means at this point. It may very well be our lot to live in the ruins. I certainly hope for something better, but I cannot predict something better. All I know is that God put us here to be lights in the darkness, and however dark it gets, our mission does not change.

Dostoyevsky wrote that stars grow brighter as the night grows darker. So the real good news is that we have the opportunity to be the brightest stars for Christ that the world has ever seen, because we may live through its darkest night.

And I think there's a real freedom to that, if you look at it a certain way. There is no reason to compromise with the world anymore, or try to fit in, or worry that we might seem weird or strange or different. We won't fit in and we will seem strange and there is no compromise. We know that now. The burdens of conformity and worldly expectations are lifted, even if they were only ever self-imposed to begin with. We should live as sore thumbs, sticking out from a mile away, and we should take joy in the fact that our culture will treat us like freaks and monsters. Every insult, every accusation, every finger pointed at us is a signpost on a lonely road, letting us know we're headed in the right direction. Whatever hardships we face for the sake of our faith should be considered pure joy, as the Book of James says.

WHERE THIS STORY IS HEADED

The line has long since been drawn in our culture. If you want to follow the wisdom of the world, stand here. If you want to follow the Word of God, stand there. And we should be standing there with God every time, in every instance, no matter what sacrifices it may require. Now we understand why Jesus called his disciples to drop everything and follow Him. It's because the world will try to load us with all sorts of baggage that will weigh us down in our pursuit of truth. We have to toss the baggage to the side and follow behind Him unburdened. There is no other way.

Few are willing to drop the baggage and live differently, as stars in a dark night, which is why there isn't much of a "war" for our culture. We lack the numbers. We are more like guerrilla warriors, scattered and depleted but continuing the fight because the only other option is surrender. And as long as even one person will hold the flag of truth and defend it, then truth is still alive, and there is light, however dim.

And, when all is said and done, we know where this story is headed. We win. Or I should say God wins. Ultimately, when the story of everything is told, the side of Truth will vanquish the side of Evil, and all who fought the good fight will be rewarded for their faith and courage. And all who abandoned their post out of fear or indifference will finally confront, with unfathomable misery, the foolishness of that decision.

We know that this is where the whole thing is going in the long run. We already took a peek at the last page and spoiled the ending for ourselves. We saw that He will wipe away every tear from our eyes and that there will be no more death or pain. We know that the Lord will come in glory. We know all of this.

We don't know what will happen in the meantime, and I suspect there is more pain to be felt and further defeats to be suffered. So be it. We will feel that pain and suffer those defeats and we will praise God all the while. I don't know how much fun we will have as the faithful remnant in a godless world, but I know we will have hope. And one day, after we have served our tour of duty on this battlefield, and fought until our last breath with courage and honor and faith, we will have our victory.

ACKNOWLEDGMENTS

Nothing I do would be possible without my wife, Alissa. She has believed in me even when I have struggled to believe in myself. She has demonstrated complete confidence in my abilities even when I so often question them. She has never laughed at my goals or told me to come down out of the clouds and be more realistic. Instead, however high I reach, she dares me to reach higher. However far I think I can go, she tells me to go even farther. She is my foundation and my purpose. A million thank-yous would never suffice, so I must apologize that this page can only fit one. Thank you.

I must thank my children, Luke and Julia (and Jeremiah, although he was safely tucked away inside his mother's womb throughout this whole endeavor). They had to sacrifice some valuable Daddy time while I shut myself in my office and typed furiously. I hope I can make it up to them.

An incredibly insufficient thank-you must go to my parents, who gave me and my five siblings an incredibly unfair advantage in life. We were never a wealthy family, but our home was rich in love and faith. Perhaps if Mom and Dad had not armed us with the truth early on, and equipped us with the tools to defend it, I would have written a very different book. I cannot take credit for being one of the few to reject our culture's lies. Mom and Dad would not have allowed anything else.

To Mary, Chrissie, Beth, Joan, and Joe: you've all influenced me in ways you'll never know. Thank you. By God's grace, let's continue to do the impossible and be a family that isn't torn apart by dysfunction, resentment, jealously, and competition. There aren't many of those left in this country. We are fortunate. Let's pray we remain so.

Thank you to Glenn Beck and *TheBlaze*. There aren't very many companies that would allow a radical flamethrower like myself to write whatever I want, without ever attempting to censor any of it, no matter how controversial or inflammatory. Glenn was an early and consistent supporter, and he continues to offer praise of my writing that far exceeds its quality. Thank you.

Thank you to my agent, Amanda Luedeke, who approached me about writing a book several years ago and stuck with me even as I spent month after month hemming and hawing and going back and forth about what sort of book I wanted to write, or if I wanted to write one at all. None of this would have been possible without her.

Thank you to the team at the Crown Publishing Group: Mary, Dave, Julia, and everyone else. Thank you for taking a chance on me, and thank you for all of the time and energy you invested in this project. This being my first book, I don't think I realized exactly how much work you guys would have to put into this thing. You have my sincere gratitude. Thank you.

Thank you to everyone I have not mentioned. Don't feel slighted by the oversight. I've become forgetful in my old age. Please forgive me.

Finally, most important, all thanks ultimately must travel upward to Our Lord in Heaven. He loves us all in ways that we do not deserve and cannot ever deserve. And nobody deserves His love and fidelity less than me. I am constantly in awe at the blessings He has bestowed on my life. And I know that every day I'm given on Earth is another challenge from Him. "Do something good and beautiful with this," He says to me, and to all of us, every morning. I know that many days have come and gone when I have not lived up to that challenge. But I must give Him all the thanks and praise that, so far, He has given me 10,000 more chances.